Best Wishes &
Buon Appetito !
Jacquelene
Miconi

Le Ricette di un Villaggio Italiano
(recipes from an Italian village)

Con Guida di Vino
(with wine guide)

by Jacqueline Miconi

Dedication

The kitchen has always occupied an important position in Italian culture. It is not only the place where cooking is done, but it's usually the center of most household activity; a place to gather and socialize, a place to bond and reminisce, and of course a place where many great chefs are born. Some of my warmest memories are associated with the kitchen, and it is from those memories and the people that were part of them, I write this cookbook.

This cookbook is dedicated to all those cooks who allowed me to watch over their shoulders, taught me what worked and what didn't, and entrusted me with some of their most secret recipes and techniques.

Thank you to my family who have instilled in me the importance of my culture and have continued to celebrate age old traditions and customs that I believe others will truly embrace.

And thank you to all those friends who have so willingly been guinea pigs for my many creations. And to my biggest critic and guinea pig of all, my husband, who has always, without hesitation, enthusiastically indulged in whatever meal I have prepared for him.

Table of Contents

Introduction

In Italy, they know that the right combination of good food, good wine and good company, are what make a great meal. For Italians, choosing the right wine for a meal is essential in enhancing the flavors of specific foods. Italy is a giant vineyard with countless varieties of wine for every taste. It is one of the world's most prolific wine producers, and is currently the top imported wine in the United States. Wine is such a large part of Italian culture, that many Italian-Americans take great pride in creating their own home-made wine, which is usually the most potent of the bunch.

Although there are some rules about matching food and wine, the final decision of the type of wine to have, lies with the tastes of the person who will be consuming it. The choices and ranges of wine in today's market place is vast and can be at times overwhelming and intimidating. Throughout this cookbook, there will be a description of many of the different types of wine available, as well as suggestions for which wines would best suit which foods.

I hope you enjoy this collection of recipes which have been developed and perfected over many years and tested by many a critical stomach. Along with the recipes and wine tips, I hope the stories and traditions throughout the cookbook help to evoke the true heritage and tastes of the Italian village.

Cooking With Wine

There are many dishes in Italian cooking that call for wine in their recipes. However, one must be sure that when using wine in a particular dish, never to buy wine marked "cooking wine" in stores, as it will take away greatly from the taste of your dish.

Be sure to purchase bottles of Red and White drinking wine, and fortified wines, such as Port, Sherry, Marsala and Vermouth at your local liquor store, to have them readily available. It is not essential for these wines to be costly, or high quality, however, it must be drinkable.

There is some leeway when you have recipes that call for certain types of wines. If you have a recipe that calls for a dry red wine, a Cabernet Sauvignon or a Merlot are the best choices. And if a recipe calls for a dry white wine, a Sauvignon Blanc or a Chardoney would taste best.

Wine is usually used in the very beginning of the cooking process, as a marinade, or at the very end as a way to 'finish off' the dish. When cooking with wine, the alcohol in the wine will evaporate at a medium simmer, and this is the goal you want to achieve. So when your dish is nearly complete, you will add your wine and then allow the dish to simmer for at least 5 minutes. This way, the tastes and aromas of the wine will not be over powering, and you will still be able to identify the distinct flavor of the wine being used.

Italian Gift Basket Ideas

Italian Coffee Lover: 2 large coffee mugs; 3 boxes Biscotti; Rock candy lollipops (to use as stirrers); Bottle of Anisette or Sambuca; can of Espresso coffee; jar powdered Cinnamon; mini Espresso cups & spoons

Pasta Lover: This or a Pasta cookbook; 2 boxes of gourmet dried pasta; string garlic bulbs; wooden spoon; jar sun-dried tomatoes; cheese grater; good quality olive oil; pasta spoon; box gourmet bread sticks

Pizza Lover: 1 large pizza stone; cheese grater; pizza cutter; Stoneware or Pizza cookbook; string garlic bulbs; sun-dried tomatoes; mini serving spatula; crushed red pepper; olive oil; pizza roller; 1 package quick-rising dry yeast

The Gourmet Italian Cook: This or another Italian cookbook; good quality vinegar; good quality olive oil; garlic press; string garlic bulbs; individual herbs (dried); 3 wooden spoons (varying sizes); jars of various marinated vegetables & olives; 2 boxes gourmet pasta; sun-dried tomatoes; Pepper mill or peppercorns

General Gifts: Espresso coffee machine; Pasta bowl set; Italian Cookbook; Boccee Ball set; Italian card set; Bottle of aged red wine; Bottle of Italian Liquor; Books about Italians/Italy; Gift Certificate to a great Italian restaurant

The Italian Kitchen

When creating a meal, no matter what the ethnic origin of it is, it is essential to always use the correct ingredients. Whether it be a fruit, vegetable, herb, meat or fish, the quality and freshness of the ingredient is important in acquiring the perfect taste. There are some very important ingredients that those who love Italian cooking should have readily available to them at all times. The following are some of the more important ingredients to help recreate an authentic taste of Italy in your own kitchen.

Herbs: Parsley, Oregano, Bay Leaves, Basil, Rosemary, Marjoram, Thyme, Italian Seasoning (These will be discussed in more detail in a later chapter)

Olive Oil: This is a light yellow to green colored oil derived from the pulp of ripe olives. It has a fruity flavor and adds a wonderful taste to any meal. This type of oil should be stored in a cool, dark place. It's varieties range from 'Extra Virgin', which is the finest and full of flavor to 'Light Virgin', which has a much more mild flavor. When choosing a type of olive oil, remember that olive oils are based on their acidity level, with the finest having the least amount of acid -- be sure to check your labels! All of the recipes in this cookbook are best created with 'Extra Virgin' olive oil, however, other varieties will do.

Balsamic Vinegar: A specialty of the Modena region in Italy, this is a richly flavored dark colored vinegar, made from the remains of certain varieties of grapes. It is wonderful in salads, as a marinade and when used in special dishes.

Parmesan Cheese: Excellent topping for many dishes, including soups, salads, pastas, stews.......and just about anything else you wish to add a little flavor to!

Garlic: This pungent herb is loved by Italians and is an essential ingredient for adding a fabulous taste and aroma to many a dish.

Tomatoes: Fresh, Canned (Crushed, Whole, Puree, Paste), Sun-dried..... they are all musts!

Olives: A small, oval oil-rich fruit of the evergreen tree usually found in the Mediterranean. Olives can be either unripe (green) or ripe (black), both with very distinct tastes. They can be served in cooking with pizza, breads, stuffings, salads, as a garnish, or as a simple finger food

Wine: Red, white, Marsala and Vermouth...all needed for either cooking or drinking

Italian Bread: A wonderful addition to every meal, especially those with savory juices, sauces or dressings....nothing beats the joy of dunking...

For the Love of Wine

This is an endless variety of wines that are consumed by Italians. The following are some of the most popular varieties, as well as a brief description and list of the best wines for the best dishes.

Reds/Rose' (Rosso)

First, there are the red wines. Some reds are light and fruity and enjoyed while young, and others are dry and tart and need to be aged for the best quality. Red wines range from medium to full-bodied in texture, and can be served with a number of dishes. This wine is to be served at room temperature.

Cabernet Sauvignon: Medium to full-bodied dry red wine; serve with meats, roasts, full flavored cheeses

Chianti: Fruity and fresh; young-serve with pasta, beef, veal; aged-serve with lamb, game and cheeses, mushrooms

Merlot: Bright ruby and fruity,soft,medium to full-bodied and easy to drink; serve with turkey, pasta, veal, cheese

Amarone: Full-bodied red; serve with cheeses, beef roasts

Barbera: Light, but tart Northern Italian dry red wine; serve with antipasto, tomato based pasta dishes, veal

Rosso di Montalcino: Medium bodied dry wine; serve with beef or pasta with a meat sauce

Bardolino: Light bodied rose'; serve with pasta salads, picnic foods, provolone, antipasti

Whites (Blanco)

Next, there are the white wines. White wines usually have a sweeter and crisper taste and are to be served chilled. Their texture ranges from light to medium-bodied and silky. Be sure to select the youngest white wine possible for the freshest taste.

Chardoney: Crisp white wine; serve with light appetizers, fish, poultry and pork, foods with cream/butter sauces

Pinot Grigio: Dry, fruity wine; serve with fish, pasta, chicken

Pinot Bianco: Fragrant, full-bodied white wine; serve with light fishes in sauce, non tomato based pasta dishes, light chicken dishes

Marino: Flavorful white wine; serve with seafood

Sauvignon Blanc: Light, dry wine; serve with mild cheeses, salads, light seafood, chicken, light soups

Soave: lean, crisp wine; serve with light fish dishes; antipasti

Sweet/Sparkling (Passiti)

Finally, there are the sparkling wines which are sweet and bubbly, and are usually served cold before meals, or with desserts

Brut Spumante: Sparkling dry wine; serve with appetizers or even very light pasta dishes

Asti Spumante: A sweet, crisp sparkling wine; serve with lightly sweet desserts or before a meal

Ice Wine: Sweet wine, smooth, satiny; serve with sweet desserts

Prosecco: Fruity,dry sparkling wine; serve with appetizers or fruit based desserts

Maslvasia: Sweet white wine; serve with cheeses or desserts

Moscato d'asti: Sweet sparkling wine; serve with light desserts

Antipasti

Served before the main course,
and usually means the dish
before the pasta dish. Most
Italian meals begin with an
appetizer course. The portions of
this course should be small and
light, and not overbearing. In
addition to the many appetizers
provided here, platters of cheese,
fruits, hams and marinated
vegetables are excellent
selections

Wines to Serve with Antipasti

The best wines to serve with antipasti dishes varies greatly. When the appetizer is a strong cheese dish, a full-bodied red wine such as a Cabernet Sauvignon is best. If you are serving a meat antipasti (such as Proscuitto), light bodied reds or roses', such as Bardolino are wonderful. When the appetizer is on the fruitier side, Prosecco, a sweet sparkling wine is best. And for the majority of other light appetizers, a dry white wine, such as a Chardoney, that is chilled with a low alcohol content or sparkling wine is best suited. Appetizers that are made with vinegar or have a large concentration of lemon juice are best served without any wine

STUFFED MUSHROOMS

2 packages large stuffing mushrooms
1/4 cup olive oil
3 cloves garlic (minced)
3/4 cup crackers
1/4 cup Italian seasoned bread crumbs
1 6 ounce can lump crab meat
4 tablespoons melted butter

Preheat oven to 375 degrees. Clean mushrooms and remove stems. Dice stems and set them aside. Take a sleeve of crackers and crumble them to a fine texture. In a large bowl, combine stems, cracker crumbs, olive oil, butter, garlic, bread crumbs and crab meat. Mix well. Add 1/4 cup of water to make the mixture cling well together. Place mushrooms in 13x9 baking dish, and place approximately 1 tablespoon of stuffing in the center of each mushroom cap. Drizzle melted butter over the top of the mushrooms. Bake uncovered for 20 minutes. Serve immediately.

Italians just like many other cultures have a variety of traditions, values and superstitions that are ingrained into their heritage. Just as cooking is a large part of Italian life, so are the cultural values that make them unique. This book would not be complete without sharing some of them......

Holy Garlic!

The Italian kitchen could not exist without the infamous garlic bulb. Garlic is a pungent herb of cloves surrounded by thin skins. Each bulb is made up of a number of pieces called cloves. This herb should be stored in a cool and dry place and should last for several months.

Many people find that mincing garlic can be both time-consuming and difficult, but there is an easy sure-fire solution. First, place the clove on a cutting board. With the flat side of a large knife, press down on clove until you hear it pop. At this point, the skin will be off, so you just discard it, and the garlic will be soft and very easy to mince. Also, the smell of garlic on your hand will be pretty strong, but it can be removed, by rubbing salt or a lemon wedge.

Along with the delicious and intriguing taste and aroma of garlic, there are also many wives tales and superstitions associated with this captivating herb. Some are:
*If you hang garlic around your neck or by windows or doors, it will ward off witches and evil spirits
*If you dream of garlic, it means Good Fortune
*If you dream of giving garlic away, it signifies bad luck
*Garlic was once believed to cure baldness and freckles!

FRIED MOZZARELLA

1 pound Mozzarella cheese
2 eggs (beaten)
1 1/2 cups Italian seasoned bread crumbs
1/2 cup Parmesan cheese
2 cups Marinara sauce
1 1/2 cups olive oil

Remove Mozzarella from package and slice into long cube-like pieces (these should appear to look like rectangles). Heat olive oil over medium/high heat. Place bread crumbs and 1/4 cup Parmesan cheese in a bowl. Mix well. Dip slices of Mozzarella in eggs, and then into bread crumb mixture, covering Mozzarella generously. Place Mozzarella in heated oil, and fry until golden brown on all sides. Place on paper towel to absorb excess oil. Serve with Marinara sauce (see page 71) and Parmesan cheese.

***For a great little picking food, try this arranged around a platter of crackers:
On a small cocktail toothpick, arrange the following: a slice of pepperoni, a marinated mushroom, a black olive, a cube of fresh Mozzarella, a roasted pepper, a green olive, a marinated mushroom and another piece of pepperoni...Not only do these look great, they taste great as well!

ROASTED PEPPERS

5 red peppers
1/2 cup olive oil
1/4 teaspoon salt
1/4 teaspoon pepper
1 clove garlic (minced)

Preheat oven to broil. Clean peppers and remove seeds. Place peppers (still whole) in baking dish, under hot broiler. Use tongs to

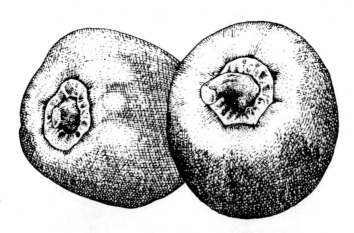

turn peppers, as each side chars and turns brown. Once peppers are browned, remove from oven and place in large bowl. Cover bowl with plastic wrap to hold in steam, and allow to sit for approximately 30 minutes. Remove cover. Peel skins off peppers, and slice longways. Add above ingredients and mix well. Serve chilled or at room temperature. Wonderful on Italian bread!

Throughout America there are many "Little Italy's" that were created by Italian immigrants who came to this country in the early 1900's and settled together in one community area. An area of the Lower East Side of New York City, holds one of the most renowned "Little Italy's" in our country. These areas are littered with restaurants, cafes and pastry shops, where the sounds, smells and tastes are truly Italian. These "Little Italy's" as we call them, are truly there own entity, where language, traditions and the culture of Italy thrive and flourish as though one were still in the 'old country'.

ZUPPA DI CLAMS FRA DIAVOLO

3 pound fresh clams (Littlenecks are best)
1 28 ounce can crushed tomatoes
1 15 ounce can chicken broth
1/4 cup dry white wine
6 cloves garlic (minced)
1 stick butter
1/4 cup olive oil
2 tablespoons hot sauce
1 tablespoon parsley
1 teaspoon crushed red pepper
1 teaspoon salt

Heat large frying pan over medium heat. Melt stick of butter. Add minced garlic, saute approximately 3 minutes. Add 1/4 cup of olive oil, hot sauce, white wine, crushed red pepper, salt, parsley, tomatoes and 1/2 can of broth (you can add some more if its too thick for your liking). Simmer 10 minutes. Add clams to mixture - cover pan, and check periodically until all clams have opened (approximately 6 minutes). Once clams have opened, this dish is ready to enjoy. Serve with Frasella or crusty Italian bread to soak up the juices.

> *Did you know that Italians believe that when entering someone's home, one must always leave through the same door they came in from, otherwise it's bad luck*

FRESH TOMATO AND MOZZARELLA SALAD

3 large tomatoes (very ripe)
1 pound fresh Mozzarella
7 fresh basil leaves
1/8 teaspoon salt
1/8 teaspoon pepper
Olive oil

Wash tomatoes and slice into circles. Layer onto a large platter. Slice fresh Mozzarella and place each piece on a slice of tomato. Chop basil leaves into 1/2" pieces and sprinkle over the top. Season with salt and pepper. Drizzle olive oil over the top. Be sure to serve balsamic vinegar on the side of this refreshing salad.

Italian Wedding Folklore

*To ward off the evil eye, on a couple's wedding day, the groom must carry a piece of iron in his pocket and the bride must cover her face with her bridal veil on her way down the aisle

*At the end of the ceremony, the couple is to shatter a glass, and the number of pieces that remain represent the number of years of a happy marriage

*In Italy, after a wedding ceremony, people in the newleywed's village would set up a sawhorse, which is a log and a double handed saw. The newlyweds would then saw the log apart with the cheering of the crowd. This tradition symbolized that the man and woman must work together in all of life's tasks

CLAMS OREGANATO

30 fresh clams (Little necks)
Bacon (10 slices, cut into 1/2" slices)
4 tablespoons olive oil
2 tablespoons butter
3 cloves garlic (minced)
2 teaspoons oregano
1/2 teaspoon salt
1/4 teaspoon pepper
3/4 cup unflavored bread crumbs
1/2 red bell pepper (diced)

Preheat oven to 425 degrees. Clean clams thoroughly and open them; discard top shells. Place bottom shell with clam inside on a

baking sheet. Heat oil and butter over low/medium heat. Add garlic (allow to saute for 2 minutes), then add red pepper, oregano, salt and pepper. Cook 6 to 7 minutes, then add bread crumbs, and cook another 3 minutes. Remove from heat. Place approximately 1 tablespoon of mixture over each clam, then a piece of bacon. Bake 12-15 minutes or until bacon is crisp. Drizzle with a little olive oil and serve.

Did you know?.... Italian cuisine varies greatly from region to region. The North is noted for their rich and creamy dishes, and the South more specifically for their hot and spicy dishes

OLIVE DIP

8 ounce bar of cream cheese

1/2 cup plain yogurt

2 small cloves garlic (minced)

3 tablespoons Parmesan cheese

1 can black olives (diced)

1/2 6 ounce jar green olives (diced)

1 teaspoon basil

1 teaspoon oregano

1/2 teaspoon black pepper

Mix all above ingredients. Serve on a platter with bread sticks, carrots, celery, zucchini sticks, etc....

MARINATED OLIVES

1 can pitted black olives

1 jar Kalamata olives

1/4 cup olive oil

1 tablespoon fresh basil

2 cloves garlic (minced)

1 tablespoon red wine vinegar

1/4 teaspoon salt

All about olives...
Black: these olives are plump with a firm, meaty texture
Green: these olives offer an earthy flavor that is firm yet juicy and salty all in one bite
Kalamata: this olive is a dark oval with an intense tart flavor

Mix all above ingredients in a medium bowl. Allow to marinate in refrigerator for 2 hours. Serve over a bed of Romaine lettuce.

ANTIPASTO SALAD

1 bunch Romaine lettuce
1/2 pound Fresh Mozzarella
1/4 pound Proscuitto
1 6 ounce can black olives
1 6 ounce jar green olives
1 12 ounce jar marinated mushrooms
1 12 ounce jar marinated eggplant
1 6 ounce jar marinated artichoke hearts
1 12 ounce jar roasted peppers (or fresh, see recipe)

Clean and tear lettuce; arrange on a large platter. Cube Mozzarella and wrap 2" slice of Proscuitto around it, and secure with a toothpick. Drain each jar of vegetables and arrange on platter, scattering throughout. Serve with balsamic vinegar and Italian bread.

The Italian flag is colored red, white and green. Each of these colors symbolize something unique about Italian culture. The green stands for the green countryside and the fruitfulness of the land, the white stands for the snow in the mountains, and the red for the bloodshed during Italy's fight for independence. However, Dante states in 'The Divine Comedies' that the colors represent the three cardinal virtues; green for hope, white for faith and red for charity.

CALAMARI SALAD

1 pound cleaned fresh calamari
1 clove garlic (minced)
1/4 cup shredded carrot
3 tablespoons fresh parsley
1/4 cup lemon juice
1/2 cup olive oil
2 tablespoons red wine vinegar
1/2 jar Mediterranean olives
Salt and Pepper to taste

Place clean calamari into a pot of boiling water for approximately 45 seconds. Remove immediately and run under very cold water to stop from cooking. Drain and pat dry. In a large mixing bowl,

combine all above ingredients, then calamari. Toss and mix well.
Serve cold with Italian bread.

Gondola rides are a staple among the canals that run through the city of Venice in Italy. Since Venice was named for the Roman Goddess Venus, it is clearly a place where romance and love filter through the air. The gondolas offer a cozy, romantic ride for travelers to experience Italy in a whole new way. And remember, if you are to go on one of these rides, take every opportunity to follow the local custom of kissing your partner as you pass under each and every bridge.

BRUSCHETTA

Bruschetta is the name for 'Italian toast'. There are a variety of toppings that can be enjoyed on this bread, however a mixture of fresh tomatoes is by far the most popular.

4 large tomatoes
2 cloves garlic (minced)
1/2 teaspoon salt
1/4 teaspoon pepper
1 tablespoon fresh basil
2 teaspoons fresh parsley

3 tablespoons olive oil
Loaf of French or Peasant bread (cut into 1/2 inch slices)

Mince garlic and saute in olive oil over low heat until soft and translucent. Remove from heat and set aside. Peel and·seed tomatoes, then dice into small pieces. Place in a large bowl, and add garlic (with oil), basil, salt and pepper. Mix well. Allow to marinate for about 1 hour in the refrigerator before serving. In a toaster oven, or under the broiler, lightly toast bread slices. Put approximately 1 tablespoon of tomato mixture on toasted bread. Drizzle with olive oil and garnish with parsley. Serve immediately. Other possible toppings for bruschetta include: chopped roasted peppers, cooked broccoli rabe with a slice of melted provolone or fried zucchini with a little Parmesan cheese.

FRIED CALAMARI

2 pounds squid (cleaned)
1 cup flour
1 cup cornmeal
2 eggs
1/2 teaspoon salt
1/2 teaspoon pepper
1 1/2 cups vegetable oil
Marinara or Cocktail sauce

Clean squid well. Place in a colandar and into the freezer for approximately 5 minutes to firm them. In a deep frying pan, heat oil over medium/high heat. Mix all above ingredients except for the eggs and the squid in a large bowl. In another bowl beat the eggs.

Next, place the calamari into the eggs, then into the flour mixture. Coat well. Drop each calamari into the hot oil and cook just under one minute, or until they are golden brown and crisp. Drain on a paper towel and serve immediately with either Marinara or Cocktail sauce or both.

Michelangelo is one of the most famous Italian artists in history. He was born in 1475 in the village of Caprese. Although he created many masterpieces throughout his life, his most famous works are the statue of David and his paintings on the arched ceiling of The Sistene Chapel in the Vatican

<u>*The Italian Table*</u>

The Italian table can easily be compared to a beautiful work of art. Platters of fresh Mozzarella and Proscuitto, servings of marinated vegetables, a bottle of aged Chianti, a loaf of crusty Italian bread....... all signatures of true Italian delicacies.

Italians take enormous pride in creating perfect dishes at every meal. Not only is the preparation and presentation of the meal important, the true satisfaction is derived from the compliments given by dinner guests. While Americans tend to serve all of the courses simultaneously, Italians prefer to separate their dishes into courses, with at times even a 'rest period' in between these courses. And remember, Italians usually serve wine before, with and after the majority of their meals.

Before an elaborate meal begins, there is usually an assortment of finger foods that are served. This part of the meal is called the antipasti, which can include an assortment of meats, marinated vegetables and fresh cheeses. Antipasti is not generally part of a family meal, but more often served at a special occasion or celebration.

Next, is the first course. This part of the meal often consists of either a soup or a simple pasta dish. It should be light and just enough to tease the palate and get you ready for the second course, which is the main part of the meal.

The second course is considered the main meal. It usually consists of a meat, fish or poultry dish, served with a side of vegetables or rice. At times, pasta is the main course, but it would usually be a heavier pasta dish, such as Fettucine Alfredo.

The third course of an Italian meal is much different than what would be expected. In many Italian families, this course consists of a simple salad, with a light balsamic vinaigrette dressing. It has been said this third course helps to aid in the digestion of foods and helps to cleanse the palate.

And finally, here in America we love our desserts. However, Italians usually do not indulge in rich desserts, unless it is a special occasion, so they will end their meal with some fruit or cheese and wine. And what would the end of a meal be without the beloved espresso coffee with either a shot of Sambucca or Anisette on the side.

Italians are definitely known for turning their meals into elaborate feasts and making the simplest of gatherings into a major occasion. But one must remember when enjoying a meal with an Italian family, the food is a mere portion of the dinner table. The atmosphere of laughter, stories, fellowship and old world traditions is what makes an Italian meal a truly memorable experience.

> "A bottle of Wine contains more philosophy than all the books in the world"
> - Louis Pasteur

Le Minestre

Soups from Italy range from delicate broths to hearty meals. It many times can be served as the opening dish, instead of a salad or pasta. When the soup is more hearty (such as Pastafagioli), it can even be served as a main meal with a loaf of warm, crusty bread and a light red wine. And the best thing about soup is that it can be served hot, warm or at room temperature

Wines to Serve with Le Minestre

When choosing a wine to serve with soup, it greatly depends on the contents of the soup. The best wines for broth based, or light vegetable soups would be a dry white wine, such as a Sauvignon Blanc, served chilled, that is slightly alcoholic. For soups that are a little heavier and tomato based, a rose' such as a Bardolino is best suited. And finally, if you are serving a hearty meat-based stew, a dry medium-bodied red wine, served at room temperature, such as a Merlot, would be best.

ITALIAN STEW

1 bunch escarole
1 medium onion (diced)
3 cloves garlic (minced)
1/4 cup olive oil
1 12 ounce can cannellini beans
1 28 ounce can crushed tomatoes
1 28 ounce can plum tomatoes
1 16 ounce can chicken broth
1 pound sweet Italian sausage
1/2 package of Ditalini pasta
1 teaspoon basil
1/2 teaspoon salt
1/8 teaspoon pepper

Clean escarole and boil until tender. Drain and set aside. In a small frying pan, brown sausage, breaking it into small pieces, then set aside. In a large sauce pan heat oil on low heat. Saute onion and garlic until translucent. Add cans of broth, crushed and plum tomatoes (be sure to tear plum tomatoes into large chunks) with all their juice. Add 2 28 ounce cans of water. Then add sausage and escarole. Add seasonings and allow to simmer on low/medium heat for approximately 45 minutes. In a separate pan, boil ditalini according to box directions, drain, then add to soup. About 10 minutes before removing from heat, add cannellini beans. Serve with warm Italian bread.

MINESTRONE

2 potatoes (peeled & cubed)

1 medium onion (diced)

2 cloves garlic (minced)

1 zucchini (peeled & diced)

2 carrots (peeled and diced)

2 large tomatoes (peeled, seeded & diced)

2 16 ounce cans chicken broth

1 16 ounce can water

1 12 ounce can kidney beans (drained)

1/2 cup olive oil

1 cup ditalini or mini shells pasta

1 tablespoon parsley

1 teaspoon oregano

1/2 teaspoon pepper
Salt to taste

In a large pan, heat olive oil over low heat. Saute onion and garlic until soft. Combine above remaining ingredients (except pasta), and simmer on medium heat for approximately 45 minutes. Keep covered, stirring occasionally. Cook pasta according to box directions, drain and add to soup about 5 minutes before soup is done. Serve with Italian bread and freshly grated Parmesan or Romano cheese.

> **Bury a mini plastic statuette of St. Joseph upside down on the front lawn if you want to sell your home**

ITALIAN WEDDING SOUP

1 bunch escarole (chopped)
1 cup carrots (chopped)
2 49 ounce cans chicken broth
1 49 ounce can water
1/2 pound ground beef
1 egg (slightly beaten)
1/2 cup Italian seasoned bread crumbs
1/4 cup Parmesan cheese
Salt & Pepper to taste
1/4 cup Parmesan cheese to garnish

In a large sauce pan, bring chicken broth and water to a boil. Add escarole and carrots, and reduce heat to medium. Allow to simmer

approximately 15 minutes. Mix ground beef, egg, bread crumbs, 1/4 cup Parmesan cheese and salt and pepper, until well blended. Form into small meatballs (like the size of large marbles) and throw them into the soup. Allow to continue simmering for another 20-25 minutes. Serve with a loaf of crusty Italian bread and the remaining Parmesan cheese.

> *Saying "Rabbit" as the first word on the first day of each month, should bring you good luck in the month to come*

<u>*How to Choose the Right Wine*</u>

In Italy, wine is a natural accompaniment to a meal. Choosing the right wine to go with a meal can many times be an anxiety provoking experience. It is known that not serving the right wine with food can easily take away from the amazing flavors of a particular dish. There are a variety of ways to choose wines to accompany certain foods.

Serving wines that have similar characteristics as the dishes they accompany is usually a good rule to follow. Elaborate and heavy dishes should be served with full-bodied wines with a strong bouquet. While lighter dishes should be served with simpler wines.

Also, one can choose a wine from the taste of a particular dish. For example when serving a sweet dessert, a sweet sparkling wine is

most suited. And when serving a heavier meat-based dish, a full-bodied red wine would do.

Wines are also many times chosen by the region in which they were created. So, many times if you are eating a dish that is a specialty of a certain area, such as Naples, a wine produced in the same area would be served.

However, ultimately the wine of choice lays in the taste buds of the individual consuming it.

PASTA e FAGIOLI

1/4 cup olive oil

3 cloves garlic (minced)

1 large prk bone (with some pork on it)

1 16 ounce can cannellini beans

1 28 ounce can tomato sauce

2 28 ounce can water

1 package ditalini pasta

5 chicken boullion cubes

1 teaspoon basil

1/4 teaspoon pepper

1/8 teaspoon salt

1/2 cup Parmesan cheese

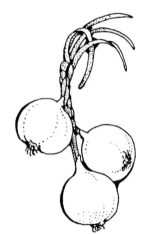

In a sauce pan, heat olive oil over low heat. Brown pork for approximately 7 minutes. Add garlic and saute about 3 minutes. Add tomato sauce, water and seasonings and allow to simmer approximately 1 hour. Add beans with all their juice and continue to simmer another 20 minutes. Cook pasta according to box directions, then add into sauce. Sprinkle Paremesan cheese over each serving. Be sure to serve this soup with some Italian bread or Italian dinner rolls.

In Italian culture, it is considered rude if one pours wine with their left hand. It is seen as an insult, and that the person for whom you are pouring wine for is not welcome in your home or in your company

CREAMY TOMATO SOUP

1 pound ripe plum tomatoes
1/2 small onion (diced)
4 tablespoons butter
1 16 ounce can chicken broth
1 16 ounce can water
1 cup light cream
1 tablespoon basil
Salt & Pepper to taste

In a soup pan, melt butter over low/medium heat. Add onion and saute for 5 minutes. Clean and chop tomatoes, then add to onions. Cook for about 5 more minutes. Add chicken broth and bring to a boil. Cover and simmer for about 10 minutes. Remove soup from the pan and place in a food processor and blend to a smooth consistency. When returning to pan, put mixture through a strainer to remove seeds and skins. Add water, cream and seasonings to soup, and simmer for approximately 10 more minutes. Reduce heat to low and keep on heat for an additional 20 minutes. Serve warm.

> "That's Amore"...Dean Martin, one of the original members of the infamous 'Rat Pack', summed up what all Italians feel about love in this wonderful song. Love is what we long for and search for our entire lives. To an Italian, a life without love is a life not worth living

ESCAROLE AND BEANS

1 bunch escarole
2 46 ounce cans chicken broth
1 46 ounce can water
1 16 ounce can cannellini beans
1 tablespoon parsley
1/4 teaspoon salt
1/8 teaspoon pepper
Romano cheese to garnish

In a large sauce pan bring chicken broth and water to a boil. Add escarole and reduce heat to medium, simmering for approximately

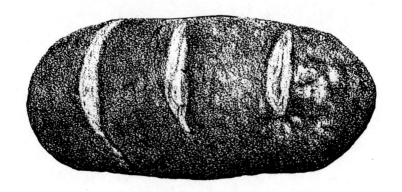

15 minutes. Add cannellini beans with all juice and seasonings; simmer another 30 minutes. Serve with Romano cheese and a loaf of Italian bread.

"La Cosa Nostra", literally meaning "This thing of ours", more commonly known in America as "The Mafia". This association of 'gentlemen' started on the island of Sicily about 500 years ago, and became more organized and developed over the years, where close-knit associates created their own form of government which included gambling, racketeering, loan sharking and a number of other illegal activities for profit

How to cook the best pasta

There are some very simple techniques one should always follow when preparing pasta, to ensure a great taste every time. You will want your pasta to be what is called "al dente" meaning "to the tooth", and not under-cooked nor over-cooked and mushy.

Pasta should always be cooked in a wide-mouth pot with approximately 3 quarts of water per pound of pasta. The pasta

will have more room to cook evenly through, than if in a smaller pot. Be sure to add salt and olive oil to the water to prevent the pasta from sticking together and also to add a little extra flavor. Before adding the pasta to the pot, be sure the water is at a full rolling boil, to help ensure that the pasta is cooked according to the time on the box directions.

Remember to taste occasionally to ensure the pasta is cooked al dente. Once tender, drain into a colander. Do not run water over pasta, it rinses away the starches that help hold a sauce onto the pasta. To help seal in the delicious flavors of your sauce you should first return the pasta to your pan. Next, ladle some of the sauce into the pan. Turn heat on the stove to low and place pan back on burner. Continue to add desired amount of sauce to pasta, stirring continuously. Remove from heat, and put pasta into your favorite serving dish, pour a little more sauce on top and serve immediately.

PANCOTTO

1 savoy cabbage
2 cloves garlic (minced)
1/2 cup olive oil
1/2 pound shredded Mozzarella cheese
1 can cannellini beans
1 28 ounce can chicken broth
1 tablespoon parsley
Salt & Pepper
1 Loaf of day-old Italian bread (cut into cubes)

Clean escarole leaves well and tear into bite size pieces. In a large pot, bring 4 quarts of water to a boil. Add escarole and cook until crisp and tender (not mushy), about 12 minutes. Drain. In a large pan, heat olive oil on low heat. Add garlic and saute for about 3 minutes. Increase heat to medium and add escarole, beans with all

juice, cheeses, bread and seasonings. Mix well and simmer for about 5 minutes, or until cheese starts to become stringy. Pour into a casserole dish and bake at 350 degrees for 30 minutes.

Those of us Italian Americans have one person to thank for 'discovering' our homeland. One of the greatest mariners in history is the Italian Christopher Columbus. He was born in 1451 in Genoa, the son of a wool merchant and weaver, who in 1492 made his famous voyage to the new land 'America'.

Pasta & Sughi

Italian pastas come in all shapes
and sizes. From spaghetti, to
penne, to ditalini, to ravioli, the
types of pasta available are vast.
Additionally, the sauces to top
these pastas are innumerable in
both taste and texture. Pasta is
versatile and can be served with
fish, meat, vegetables or baked in
the oven. It is traditionally
another option for a first course,
when served as a smaller portion.
However, pasta in any form can
be served as a meal.

Wines to Serve with Pasta & Sughi

Since pasta is so versatile, the types of wine to serve with this dish depends greatly on the sauce served with the pasta. For a light pasta dish with olive oil or pesto, Sparkling dry wine like Brut Spumante is great. When serving a pasta with a meat or tomato sauce, light to medium-bodied red wines such as a Merlot or Barbera are perfect. For pasta with light fish sauces, light whites, such as a Sauvignion Blanc are ideal. For those heavier seafood sauces, dry, full-bodied whites such as Pinot Grigio are well suited. And for those creamy pasta dishes, a stong, full-bodied white wine like a Pinot Bianco is great.

PASTA PRIMAVERA

2 cloves garlic (minced)
1 small onion (diced)
1 yellow squash (peeled & diced)
1 zucchini (peeled & diced)
1 cup broccoli florets
1/2 cup peas
1/4 cup olive oil
1/2 can plum tomatoes (torn apart)
1 16 ounce can chicken broth
1/2 cup heavy cream
1/2 cup Parmesan cheese
1 box angel hair/thin spaghetti

In a large pan, warm olive oil over low/medium heat. Saute onion and garlic for approximately 3 minutes. Add remaining vegetables and continue to saute over medium heat for an additional 10-15 minutes, or until vegetables are tender. Add 3/4 can of broth and cream. Slowly add Parmesan cheese, stirring continuously. Allow to thicken (approximately 5 minutes). Boil pasta according to box directions and mix immediately with sauce. If sauce seems pasty or too thick to your liking, add some of remaining chicken broth until it reaches desired consistency.

> When in dire need of prayers for the sick, dead or dying, go to church and light a candle for that individual

PESTO SAUCE

4 cloves garlic (minced)
2 cups fresh basil leaves (chopped)
3/4 cup parsley
2/3 cup Pine nuts
1 1/2 cups Parmesan cheese
1 1/2 cups olive oil

Place garlic, basil, parsley, pine nuts and Parmesan cheese in blender. Blend at medium speed for approximately 2 minutes. Continue blending on a low speed, while adding oil slowly until smooth. The consistency of this sauce will be somewhat pasty. Since the sauce is not heated, you will serve this over a hot pasta, such as fettucine or bow ties.

> *In Rome lies probably the greatest amphitheater in history, The Colosseum. It was created under the Emperor Vespasian from 72 to 81 A.D. and consists of 3 and 1/2 million tons of stone. It was mostly used as a place of entertainment, where criminals were punished, eccentrics of the time (jugglers, mimes, etc...) would perform, and where great fights between gladiators and ferocious animals would take place.*

CRAB SAUCE ALL' AMALFITANA

2 28 ounce cans crushed tomatoes
2 tablespoons fresh parsley (chopped)
1 clove garlic (minced)
1/2 cup olive oil
1 1/2 cups water
6 hard shell crabs (if not fresh, Frozen Blue Crabs are best)
Salt & Pepper to taste

In a large sauce pan, heat olive oil on low/medium heat. Saute garlic for about 3 minutes, then add crabs and continue to simmer for 10 minutes. Add tomatoes, water, parsley, salt and pepper. Once sauce begins to simmer, turn heat to low and cook for 45 minutes. Serve over linguine or spaghetti.

Another taste of Italian Wedding Folklore...

*On her wedding day, the Italian bride should not wear any gold jewelry, it is thought to bring bad luck, until of course the wedding band is on
*Like today, the bride carries a satin bag called a 'la borsa', where guests place envelopes containing money to help pay for the wedding and to help start the couple's future together

Those Wonderful Herbs

There are a variety of herbs used in Italian cooking. They each have their own distinct aroma and flavor, and are an integral part of many a dish. Remember, if you are using dried herbs, you will not always use as much, because they are much more potent than fresh herbs. The following is a brief description of the most popular herbs used and the dishes in which they are most suited for:

BASIL: a robust, pungent herb with a spicy aroma. Great with: salads; sauces; pizza; eggplant; zucchini; pasta dishes

BAY LEAVES: "sweet laurel"; Native to the Mediterranean region. Wonderful taste when used fresh, but always remember to remove leaf before serving. Great with: meats; roasted chicken; broths; stews; soups

MARJORAM: resembles oregano, but more subtle and slightly sweeter. Great with: salads; meatloaf; fish; scones and when added to olive oil for dipping

OREGANO: a robust and aromatic herb with a strong concentrated flavor. Great with: salads; tomato based sauces; pizza; casseroles; soups; vegetables and pasta dishes

PARSLEY: herb with a mild, crisp flavor. Be sure to get Italian parsley and not curly parsley. Great with: casseroles; soups; salads; fish; tomatoes; chicken; eggplant

ROSEMARY: a strong, distinctive herb, with leaves that have a piney flavor and resemble pine needles. Discard whole sprig before serving. Great with: lamb; roasts; chicken; veal; pork; potatoes

THYME: strong herb with a great flavor that intensifies as you cook it. Just a pinch is needed for most recipes. Great with: meat mixtures; roasts; marinades; stuffings

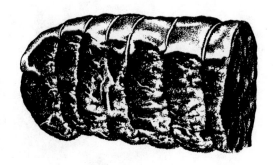

WHITE CLAM SAUCE

3 cloves garlic (minced)

2 tablespoons fresh parsley (chopped)

1/4 cup shallots (chopped)

1/4 cup olive oil

3 tablespoons butter

1/2 cup white wine

1 16 ounce can chicken broth

1 pound Little neck clams (cleaned)

Parmesan cheese to taste

In a sauce pan, heat olive oil and butter together over low/medium heat. Saute garlic and shallots for approximately 5 minutes. Add white wine and broth, and simmer for an additional 5 minutes. Stir in parsley and clams and bring to a light boil. Reduce heat and simmer for 15 minutes. The clams should open after about 7 minutes, but continue to simmer. Serve immediately over hot pasta (linguine, spaghetti or capellini are best) Serve with grated Parmesan cheese.

Italians believe that odd numbers are always luckier... with anything and everything.... from the number of glasses of wine you consume, to the number of children you have!

Italian Coffee

What is a day in the life of an Italian like without the beloved cup of Espresso, or another version of this rich, dark coffee? Italians usually drink this coffee at some time during the day, however, it is never served with a meal, only before or after it. Remember, having a cup of steaming espresso or creamy cappuccino with some light dessert is a wonderful way to create a relaxing atmosphere at the conclusion of your meal; it allows the stories, laughter and fellowship shared at the Italian table to linger just a little longer....

Espresso: this is a very strong, black coffee that is a pleasure indulged in daily by most Italians. This coffee is many times served with Anisette or Sambuca liquor on the side and a twist of lemon. This coffee should be served very hot.

Caffe' Latte: this is usually served as an Italian breakfast coffee since it is somewhat lighter than straight Espresso. This coffee is usually equal parts of Espresso coffee and steamed milk, which has been "frothed", and should also be served very hot.

Cappuccino: this coffee is the least strong of them all. It is one part Espresso and two parts steamed milk. This coffee should also be served very hot, and is usually topped with some powdered cocoa or cinnamon for a little extra flavor.

*Remember when serving Sambuca with Espresso; it is usually served in a snifter glass, and must be served with 3 coffee beans in it. Of course 3 being an odd number is good luck, and also to many Italians 3 symbolizes the Holy Trinity: The Father, The Son & The Holy Spirit

CHICKEN AND BROCCOLI ALFREDO

1 1/2 cups fresh broccoli florets (chopped)
1 small onion (diced)
2 cloves garlic (minced)
1 pound skinless chicken breasts (cleaned)
2 chicken bouillon cubes
1/2 stick butter
1 cup light cream
1/2 cup water
1/4 cup white wine
3/4 cup fresh grated Parmesan cheese
1/2 teaspoon salt
1/4 teaspoon pepper
1 box Fettuccine

In a large skillet, heat butter over medium heat. Brown chicken on both sides, and remove from pan. Reduce heat and add garlic and onion. Saute for approximately 5 minutes. Stir in broccoli and saute until tender (about 7 minutes). Cut cooked chicken into chunks and add back to pan. Add water, cream and wine, then stir in Parmesan cheese slowly. Bring to a light boil, and add bouillon cubes, salt and pepper, and simmer for approximately 10 minutes. Cook pasta according to box directions and pour Alfredo sauce over top. Serve immediately.

Never give pearls as a present, they are to be inherited ONLY!

VEGETABLE LASAGNA

1 zucchini (diced)

1 16 ounce bag fresh spinach

1 bunch broccoli (chopped)

1 small onion (diced)

5 large tomatoes (peeled, seeded, chopped)

1 clove garlic (minced)

1/2 16 ounce can black olives (diced)

1 egg

2 pound container Ricotta cheese

12 ounce bag Mozzarella cheese

1/2 cup Parmesan cheese

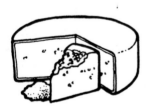

1/2 cup olive oil
1/8 teaspoon of the following: salt, pepper, oregano & basil
1 box lasagna noodles

In a small sauce pan, bring 5 cups water to a boil. Add spinach and boil for 10 minutes. Drain and set aside. In a large skillet, heat olive oil over low/medium heat. Add zucchini, broccoli, onion, garlic, tomatoes and black olives, and saute for approximately 10 minutes. Remove from heat and add spinach and seasonings to vegetable mixture. In a large bowl, mix egg, Ricotta, Mozzarella cheese and Parmesan cheese. In a large sauce pan, bring 3 quarts water to a boil and cook lasagna noodles according to box directions, drain and run under cold water until cooled. In a large lasagna pan or deep baking dish, ladle some

VEGETABLE LASAGNA (con't)

mixture onto bottom of pan. Layer noodles long ways to cover the bottom of pan. Then layer: mixture of vegetables, mixture of cheeses, then lasagna noodles. Continue doing this until all lasagna noodles are gone (this should make 2 or 3 layers). The top layer should be lasagna noodles. Cover and Bake on 350 degrees for 45-50 minutes. Allow to cool for about 15 minutes before cutting and serving.

CREAMY HERB SAUCE

1 cup whipping cream
1/4 cup Parmesan cheese
3 shallots (diced)
1 clove garlic (minced)
2 teaspoons basil
2 teaspoons parsley
2 tablespoons olive oil
Salt & Pepper to taste

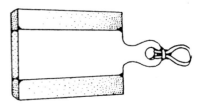

In a small pan heat olive oil over low heat. Add shallots and garlic and saute for about 5 minutes. Increase heat to medium and add all remaining ingredients except Parmesan cheese. Simmer for 15 minutes, decreasing temperature if it comes to a boil. Serve over bow tie pasta, and top with Parmesan cheese.

SUNDAY GRAVY (MEAT BASED MARINARA SAUCE)

This tomato sauce with meat is called gravy, because the meat drippings become the base for the sauce.

1 pound of the following: pork, beef, sausage
3 cans crushed tomatoes
2 cans plum tomatoes (torn in large pieces)
1 medium onion (diced)
3 cloves garlic (minced)
5 fresh basil leaves (chopped)
2 fresh oregano sprigs (chopped)
1/2 cup olive oil
6 cups water
1/2 teaspoon sugar
Salt & Pepper to taste

Clean and trim fat off pork and beef. In a large sauce pan, warm oil on medium heat. Add meats and brown on all sides. Once browned, remove from pan and set aside. Reduce heat to low, and allow oil to cool (about 5 minutes). Add onion and garlic and saute for approximately 5 minutes. Add remaining ingredients and cook at a light boil for about 20 minutes. Return meats to the pan and allow to simmer on low heat for 2 1/2 - 3 hours.

> *Did you lose something important to you?*
> *Italians believe if you pray to Saint*
> *Anthony, you will recover it*

SPINACH RAVIOLI

<u>Dough:</u> *3 cups flour, 1/2 teaspoon salt, 2 eggs, 1 cup warm water*
<u>Filling:</u> *1 large package fresh spinach (chopped), 2 pound container Ricotta cheese, 1/2 cup Parmesan cheese, 1 12 ounce package Mozzarella cheese, 2 egg yolks, 1 tablespoon parsley, 1/2 teaspoon ground nutmeg, 1/4 teaspoon salt & pepper*

First prepare the dough: Sift flour and salt. Add eggs and mix well. Slowly add water and knead until smooth. Cover and set aside for 30 minutes. Then split dough evenly in half, and roll out each on a floured surface until very thin.

Next, prepare the filling: In a medium sauce pan, bring 3 quarts of water to a boil. Add spinach and boil until tender (about 10 minutes), drain and set aside. In a large bowl, mix all above filling

ingredients until smooth.

Next, place approximately 1 teaspoon of filling on one dough sheet, about 1 1/2 inches apart from each other. Place the other sheet of dough on top. Gently press with fingertips around each teaspoon of filling. Cut into squares with a pastry cutter. Allow ravioli to dry out for 1 hour. In a large pan, bring 4 quarts of water to a boil. Add ravioli. Cook for approximately 10-15 minutes or until tender. Serve with Marinara sauce and grated Parmesan.

The Mona Lisa, which is probably the world's most famous painting was created by Italian Leonardo da Vinci, and was started in 1503 and completed in 1506

PENNE ALLA VODKA

1/4 cup olive oil

1/2 stick butter

2 cloves garlic (minced)

2 pieces Prosciutto (chopped)

5 sundried tomatoes (chopped)

1/2 cup Vodka

1/2 cup heavy cream

2 tablespoons fresh parsley

1/2 teaspoon crushed red pepper

1/2 28 ounce can crushed tomatoes

1/2 cup Parmesan cheese

1 box penne pasta

Cut prosciutto into small bite size pieces. In a large frying pan, heat olive oil and butter and saute prosciutto and garlic until lightly browned. Add tomatoes (both), parsley, salt and pepper and allow to simmer for about 15 minutes. Next add Vodka and heavy cream and continue simmering for another 20-25 minutes, so that alcohol can cook off. Cook penne according to box directions and drain. Add penne pasta one scoop at a time to the Vodka sauce stirring continuously. Add Parmesan cheese and serve. For a wonderful addition to this dish, make chicken cutlets, then slice into pieces and throw into sauce before mixing it with the pasta.

If you wish to ward off rain, be sure to take any statues of Saints you have and place them facing outward in a window sill

GEMELLI AND BROCCOLI

3 cups broccoli florets
4 cloves garlic (minced)
1/2 large white onion (diced)
4 tablespoons butter
1 tablespoon olive oil
1/2 cup white wine
3/4 cup Parmesan cheese
1 pound Gemelli pasta
Salt & Pepper to taste

In a large pot, bring 4 quarts of water to a rolling boil. Add pasta and cook according to box directions. Drain and return to large pot, stirring in 2 tablespoons of butter. In a small pan, simmer broccoli in about 1 quart of water for about 7 minutes or until tender. Drain and set aside. In a frying pan, heat remaining butter and olive oil over low/medium heat. Add onions and garlic and saute for about 5 minutes. Then add broccoli, wine and salt and pepper and simmer an additional 10 minutes. Add broccoli mixture to pasta and stir. Add Parmesan cheese, mixing thoroughly and serve immediately.

Put brand new shiny coins on the window sill before midnight on New Years Eve, and you will be guaranteed good luck in the year to come

<u>*Popular Italian Proverbs*</u>

**Meglio tardi che mai:*
  Better late than never
***Amico di tulti e di nessuno e' tutt'uno:*
  A friend to all, is a friend to none
***Tal Padre, 'al figlio:*
  Like father, like son
***Sfortuna al gioco, fortuna in amore:*
  Unlucky at cards, lucky in love
***L'appetito vien mangiando:*
  Appetite comes with eating
***Finche c'e'vita c'e'speranza:*
  As long as there is life, there is hope
***Il tempo e' un gran medico:*
  Time is a great healer

**L'abito non fa it monaco*
  The habit doesn't make the monk
**Chi cerca trova*
  Who searches, finds
**Non domandare all'oste se ha buon vino*
  Don't ask the host if he has good wine
**Non si puo avere la botte piena e la moglie ubriaca*
  You can't have a full bottle and a drunken wife
  American translation: You can't have your cake and eat it too

Pesce

The Italians love their fish!
Being surrounded by water on
three sides, fish is an integral
part of the Italian diet, with
countless recipes enjoyed
throughout the various regions
of Italy. Succulent seafood
dishes can be prepared in many
ways, with a variety of
seasonings, rices and vegetables

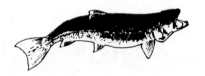

Wines to Serve with Pesce

There are a variety of wines that are a great accompaniment to seafood dishes. For light seafood dishes, such as baked, steamed or grilled fish, a crisp, dry full-bodied white wine, served very cold, like a Soave is great. For a heavier seafood dish, light red wines like Barbera, or full-bodied white wines like Pinot Grigio are preferable. And for shellfish, strong white wines like a Marino are best. Remember when choosing your white wines, those that are youngest have the freshest taste.

SHRIMP PIZZAIOLA

2 pounds jumbo shrimp
1 28 ounce can plum tomatoes (torn into bite size pieces)
1 cup peas
3 tablespoons olive oil
3 cloves garlic (minced)
1/4 cup water
1/2 teaspoon salt
1/4 teaspoon pepper
1/2 teaspoon basil
1/2 teaspoon oregano
Parmesan cheese to garnish

In a large skillet, warm olive oil on low/medium heat. Add garlic and saute for approximately 5 minutes. Add tomatoes, water, seasonings and peas. Simmer for about 25 minutes. Preheat oven to 375 degrees. Rinse, shell, devein and butterfly shrimp. Place shrimp in a baking dish, and top with sauce. Bake for 10 minutes. Serve with pasta or rice. Garnish with Parmesan cheese.

Traditionally, Italian women stayed at home, while their husbands were the bread winners. And even though many Italian women now work outside the home, home is still seen where one's most important work takes place. It is the central domain where the Italian woman works on maintaining balance, love and harmony and keeps the family unit functioning

SHRIMP FLORENTINE

1 pound jumbo shrimp (cleaned, shelled & deveined)
2 16 ounce bags fresh spinach
1 egg
1 1/2 cups flour
1 16 ounce can chicken broth
1/4 cup lemon juice
1/2 cup dry white wine
1/4 cup olive oil
3 tablespoons butter

1/4 teaspoon of parsley, salt & pepper
Lemon wedges for garnish

In a small bowl beat 2 eggs. Place flour in another small bowl. In a large skillet, warm olive oil and butter on medium heat. Dip cleaned shrimp in egg, then into flour. Fry until lightly browned on both sides. Once done, set shrimp aside. Meanwhile, boil spinach in 4 quarts of water in a large pan until tender (about 10 minutes). When done, drain and set aside. In the large skillet, add remaining ingredients. Simmer for about 5 minutes. Reduce heat to low, then add shrimp back to mixture and allow to cook an additional 10 minutes. To thicken juice in pan, mix 1 tablespoon butter and 2 tablespoons of flour (blend well), and add a little at a time, stirring continuously until desired thickness is reached. Place spinach on a large serving platter, and pour shrimp mixture over the top. Serve immediately. Great with Risotto on the side!

ITALIAN SHELLFISH KABOBS

1 zucchini (cut in chunks)
1 yellow squash (cut in chunks)
1 red pepper (cut in 1/2" squares)
2 cloves garlic (minced)
1/4 cup fresh parsley (chopped)
1 pound fresh shrimp (cleaned, peeled & deveined)
1 pound fresh sea scallops
2 cups Italian style bread crumbs
1/2 cup olive oil
4 tablespoons butter
1/4 cup Parmesan cheese
1/4 teaspoon salt
1/8 teaspoon pepper
1 package Arborio rice
1 package skewers

In a large bowl, combine bread crumbs, Parmesan cheese and olive oil. Mix well. Add shrimp and scallops, and toss to coat fish evenly. Leave in bowl and cover and refrigerate about a half hour. Meanwhile, cook rice according to package directions and set aside. In a large skillet, melt butter and saute garlic about 3 minutes. Then stir in rice, parsley, salt and pepper. Next, place seafood and vegetables (zucchini, squash, red pepper) on skewers and broil about 10 minutes, turning frequently. Serve over Risotto rice with lemon wedges on side.

SEAFOOD RISOTTO

1 28 ounce can chicken broth

1 1/2 cups Arborio rice

1 pound mixed raw seafood (shrimp, clams, calamari- all cleaned)

1 stalk celery (minced)

1 carrot (minced)

3 cloves garlic (minced)

1/2 cup Parmesan cheese

1/2 teaspoon salt

1 teaspoon parsley

1/4 teaspoon oregano

1/4 teaspoon pepper

In a large pan, bring broth to a boil. Add rice and cook according to box directions. Drain and save excess liquid. In a large skillet, warm butter on medium heat. Saute celery and carrot for approximately 8 minutes, then add garlic and saute an additional 3 minutes. Add seafood and continue to cook until clams have opened. Once clams open, remove clams from shells, discard shells and return clams to the pan. Next, add rice to the seafood mixture and simmer about 5 minutes. Remove from heat and stir in Parmesan cheese, then add 1/4 cup of the left over liquid from the rice. Serve immediately.

> *Italians believe that when passing a church or a graveyard, one must always give the sign of the cross.*

"*The Italian Solution*"

There is nothing better than a story being passed down among families and generations. Throughout my life, I have heard countless tales of how family members have dealt with various life situations. Many times I have been left asking myself 'What

were they thinking?' It just seems to be true that Italians sometimes have their own solutions to everyday trials and tribulations. The following stories are just too good to be forgotten....

In the early 1950's, when my mother and aunt (her twin sister) were young children, my grandmother had a perfect solution when she was in need of a babysitter. Whenever she had a lot of work to do around the house, and no one to watch her girls, she would take pieces of rope, tie it around their waists and strap them to the clothesline, so they would still be able to run around the backyard. Apparently, they loved this, and there is home movies of them running into each other and getting tangled. Imagine your neighbor seeing this in your backyard today....

This is a favorite story among my husband's family about his grandfather. His grandfather made his own home-made wine, which he believed he would put to good use.
 What he would do is this: In an effort to capture his own food for meals, he would take some Italian bread, soak it in his wine and throw it in the backyard. Eventually, the blackbirds would come and eat the bread, get drunk, and topple over. At this

time, he would collect them, and Vwalah! cooked blackbirds. Grandpa Miconi enjoyed his blackbirds for quite a while, until some nosey neighbors informed the Health Department.....

There are many stories we have all heard about ways some Italians have earned extra money. Well this one comes from the town of Amalfi in Italy where my grandmother's family is from. In the early 1900's, Italy had a very unique "foster care" system. Whenever Amalfitans were in need of extra money, they would head down to the town orphanage. Once there, children were put on a type of conveyer belt, and were chosen to be cared for that day. When the child was returned in the evening, the person who cared for the child would be given some money. This system of care eventually led to the adoption of my grandmother's brother, whom my great-grandmother had become very attached to.

An individual's home has more hiding places that one could imagine. And with a little forethought, my husband's grandfather, who didn't believe in the banking system, would hide money everywhere throughout his house. He would remove light switches, tie strings to wires in the wall, and lower money down into the walls. He would put money in jars, and then into large barrels of wine; the only give away would be that whenever he would give this money to anyone, they would always be greeted with that potent and distinct smell of his wonderful wine.

Carne & Pollo

A meat or chicken dish, is
usually the traditional second
course of an Italian meal. These
entrees can be prepared in a
wide variety of ways. The
distinctive Italian seasonings
used with these dishes result in
hearty and savory meals. And
incorporating fresh vegetables,
only adds to the intense flavors
of the following recipes.

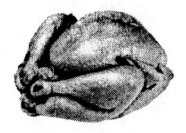

Wines to serve with Carne & Pollo

There are many different wines that suit the variety of meat and chicken dishes that are created in the Italian kitchen. Beef dishes are best served with strong, full-bodied dry red wines, like Amarone, Cabernet Sauvignon, or a young Chianti. For chicken dishes served in sauces, medium-bodied reds, like a Merlot is great. Light chicken dishes are best served with a crisp, light white wine, like a Chardoney that is served very cold. Veal is best suited with soft, fruity red wines, like a young Chianti or a medium-bodied Merlot. And finally, pork dishes are best served with a light red, like a Bardolino or a crisp white wine like a Chardoney.

CHICKEN ISCANTANO

1 1/2 pounds boneless chicken breasts (cleaned)
1/2 small onion
1 12 ounce package white mushrooms (sliced)
1 cup olive oil
1 egg
1/4 cup milk
1 stick butter
1 16 ounce can artichoke hearts (sliced)
1 16 ounce can chicken broth
1/4 cup Marsala wine
Salt & pepper to taste

In a large skillet, warm olive oil over medium heat. In a small bowl, beat egg and milk together, and sprinkle some salt and pepper. Place flour in a separate small bowl. Dip chicken pieces into egg, then flour, and place in skillet. Cook chicken until well browned on both sides. Remove chicken from pan. Add mushrooms and onion to pan and saute approximately 5 minutes. Drain olive oil out of pan. Add butter and artichoke hearts and saute about 10 more minutes. Return chicken to pan. Add 1/2 can of chicken broth and Marsala wine, and allow to simmer an additional 15 minutes. Serve immediately with a side of plain capellini or spaghetti. The sauce from this dish is wonderful over pasta.

ITALIAN BEEF STEW

1 1/2 pounds stewing beef
1 medium onion (sliced longways)
2 cloves garlic (minced)
1 28 ounce can plum tomatoes (torn in pieces)
3 large potatoes (peeled & chopped)

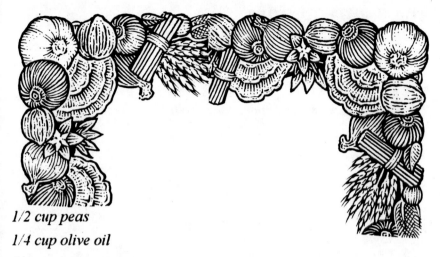

1/2 cup peas
1/4 cup olive oil
1/4 cup water
1/2 teaspoon salt
1/4 teaspoon pepper
1/4 teaspoon basil
1/8 teaspoon oregano

In a large skillet, warm olive oil on low/medium heat. Add beef and brown on all sides. Then add onion and garlic and saute about 5 minutes. Remove from heat. Preheat oven to 375 degrees. Next, place meat with onion, garlic and all juices in a 9x13 baking dish. Add tomatoes, water and seasonings. Cover tightly and cook for 2 hours. Add potatoes and peas and cook for an additional hour. The stew is many times served over rice/risotto, but is just as good served with a loaf of crusty Italian bread.

> When making a toast, most
> Italians will end it with "Salute",
> which means "Good health to all"

CHICKEN CACCIATORE

2 pounds chicken legs & thighs
1 large onion (cut in strips)
1 12 ounce package white mushrooms (sliced)
1 red pepper (cut into strips)
2 cloves garlic (minced)
1 28 ounce can plum tomatoes (torn in pieces)
3 tablespoons olive oil
1/2 cup dry white wine
1 16 ounce can chicken broth
1 tablespoon parsley
1/2 teaspoon oregano
1/4 teaspoon pepper
1/8 teaspoon salt
1 package egg noodles (if desired)

In a large skillet, warm olive oil over medium heat. Sprinkle salt
and pepper and dust of flour on chicken and fry until well

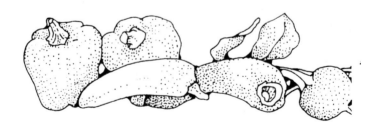

browned. Remove chicken from pan. Add garlic, onion, red pepper and mushrooms, and saute for 10 minutes. Place chicken back in pan and add all remaining ingredients. Once a light boil begins, reduce heat to low, so its just simmering, and cover partially. Cook for 1 1/2 hours, stirring occasionally. If desired, boil egg noodles according to box directions and serve cacciatore over the top.

VEAL MARSALA

1 1/2 pounds veal cutlets (cleaned & sliced thin)
1 12 ounce package white mushrooms (sliced)
3 cloves garlic (minced)
4 tablespoons butter
1/4 cup olive oil
1/2 cup Marsala wine
1 16 ounce can chicken broth
Flour to dust
Salt & pepper to taste

In a large, deep frying pan, heat olive oil and butter on low/medium heat. Dust each piece of veal with flour and cook until lightly browned on both sides. Once browned, remove from pan. Add mushrooms and garlic and saute for approximately 7 minutes. Place veal back in the pan and add Marsala wine and 1/2 can of chicken broth. Reduce heat to low, and allow to simmer for 20 minutes. To thicken sauce, mix 1 tablespoon of butter and 2 tablespoons of flour. Add gradually to pan, stirring continuously, until sauce reaches desired thickness. Serve with a loaf of Italian bread, to soak up the tasty juices.

An old tradition that is still observed in many Italian families, is that the oldest gentleman at the table (usually the grandfather) is always served first, then the rest of the family may eat.

SAUSAGE & PEPPERS

1 pound sweet Italian sausage (sliced into cubes)
3 green peppers (sliced longways)
2 red peppers (sliced longways)
1 large onion (sliced longways)
1 28 ounce can crushed tomatoes
3 cloves garlic (minced)
1/2 cup olive oil
4 fresh basil leaves (chopped)
2 sprigs oregano (chopped)
1/4 teaspoon salt
1/8 teaspoon pepper
1 loaf Italian bread

In a large skillet, heat olive oil on medium heat. Add peppers and onions and saute for 15 minutes or until tender. Add garlic, tomatoes and seasonings and continue to simmer an additional 10 minutes. In another small skillet, fry sausage on medium heat until browned (about 7 minutes). Next, add sausage to large skillet and mix well. Continue to simmer about 10 more minutes. Serve with a loaf of warm Italian bread.

> *As my aunt would always say when she was aggravated; 'Jesus, Mary & Joseph'; somehow Italians feel better about saying words of religious significance than anything different*

MEATBALLS & STRINGBEANS

1 pound ground beef
1 1/2 pounds green string beans (cleaned)
1/2 cup Italian seasoned bread crumbs
1/4 cup Parmesan cheese
1/2 cup olive oil
1 egg
1/2 teaspoon oregano
1/2 teaspoon basil
1/4 teaspoon thyme
1/4 teaspoon salt
1/8 teaspoon pepper
3 cups Marinara sauce (see page 71)
Loaf of Italian bread

In a large bowl, combine ground beef, bread crumbs, Parmesan cheese, egg and seasonings. Mix well. In a large skillet, heat

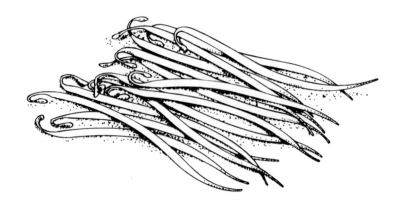

olive oil over medium heat. Form meat mixture into balls about 2 inches in diameter. Add to olive oil and fry until well browned on all sides. Once done, set aside on towel paper to drain excess oil. Meanwhile, in a medium pan, bring about 3 cups of water to a boil. Add string beans and simmer for 10 minutes or until fork tender. Drain and set aside. In another saucepan, heat Marinara sauce on low/medium heat. Add string beans. Simmer about 5 minutes. Next, break up meatballs into large bite size pieces and add to sauce and string beans. Heat for another 10 minutes.

ITALIAN POT ROAST MARINADE

4 pounds beef for pot roast (chuck or brisket)
1 large onion (sliced)
2 large carrots (peeled & diced)
1 zucchini (peeled & diced)
1 stalk celery (diced)
4 cloves garlic (minced)
2 tablespoons butter
1/2 cup olive oil
1 cup dry red wine
1 tablespoon parsley
1/2 teaspoon oregano
1/2 teaspoon salt
1/4 teaspoon pepper

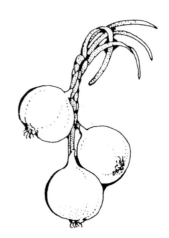

About 6-8 hours before cooking (or longer if desired), marinate the beef with olive oil, wine, garlic and seasonings. Cover and place in refrigerator. Preheat oven to 350 degrees. In a large roasting pan, place pot roast with marinade and remaining vegetables. Cover and cook for about 3 hours or until fork tender.

The orange blossom is the most traditional flower used in Italian weddings both past and present. This flower is many times worn in the bride's hair or in her bouquet and represents purity and chastity

CHICKEN & BROCCOLI RABE

1 pound boneless skinless chicken breasts (cleaned)
2 bunches broccoli rabe
1/2 cup olive oil
1 small onion (diced)
2 cloves garlic (minced)
1 16 ounce can Chicken broth
1/3 cup Parmesan cheese
1/2 teaspoon salt
1/4 teaspoon pepper

In a large, deep skillet, bring 5 cups water to a boil. Trim 2 inches from the bottom of broccoli rabe stems and discard. Add broccoli rabe and cook for 12 minutes or until tender. Once cooked, drain well and add olive oil, garlic and onion to pan. Reduce heat to low and simmer for 5 minutes. Take off burner and cover to keep warm. Next, broil (or grill) chicken until done, turning frequently, so not to dry it out. Place skillet with broccoli rabe back on stove on medium heat, and add chicken and chicken broth. Allow to simmer 10 minutes. Serve immediately. Garnish with Parmesan cheese.

> In Ancient Rome, the 6th day of the week was dedicated to the beautiful Goddess Venus. Eventually the day became Friday, and was then considered the luckiest day of the week

ITALIAN STUFFED CHICKEN BREASTS

2 pounds boneless skinless chicken breasts

1 12 ounce package white mushrooms (sliced)

1/4 cup olive oil

1 10 ounce package frozen spinach (thawed & drained)

3 cloves garlic (minced)

1/2 teaspoon crushed red pepper, oregano & salt

1/4 cup Parmesan cheese

1 cup Marsala wine

1/2 cup Italian seasoned bread crumbs
1/2 teaspoon cornstarch
2 tablespoons water

Heat 2 tablespoons oil over medium heat. Saute garlic for approximately 4 minutes. Add pepper, salt, oregano and spinach. Cook for about 5 minutes. Put this mixture in a medium bowl and add 2 tablespoons of Marsala wine and Parmesan cheese. Mix well. Place about 2 tablespoons of spinach mixture in center of chicken. Roll and secure with toothpicks. Dredge chicken into bread crumbs, coating thoroughly. Heat remainder of oil over medium heat and cook chicken thoroughly. Remove chicken and set aside. Add mushrooms and saute until soft. Add Marsala wine to pan and allow to simmer for 5 minutes. In a small bowl mix cornstarch and water, then add to pan. Return chicken to pan, reduce heat to low and simmer about 10 more minutes.

CHICKEN WITH LEEKS

1 1/2 pounds boneless skinless chicken breasts
1 cup fresh leeks (chopped)
2 28 ounce cans plum tomatoes (torn into bite size pieces)
1/2 cup olive oil
4 tablespoons butter
1/2 cup dry Vermouth
1/2 cup fresh grated Parmesan cheese
1/2 teaspoon salt
1/2 teaspoon basil
1/4 teaspoon thyme
1/4 teaspoon pepper
1/2 pound angel hair pasta

In a large skillet, warm olive oil and butter on medium/high heat. Fry cleaned breasts until browned on both sides and cooked

almost through (about 12 minutes). Remove chicken and set side. Turn heat to low/medium, and place leeks in pan and saute for 5 minutes. Add tomatoes with all their juice. Add Vermouth and seasonings and let simmer an additional 10 minutes. Cut chicken into large chunk like pieces and return to pan. Reduce heat to low and simmer for 30 minutes. Serve over angel hair pasta with a generous amount of Parmesan cheese.

NEAPOLITAN PORKCHOPS

6 porkchops (3/4 - 1 inch thick)
1 12 ounce package white mushrooms
2 green peppers (cleaned & chopped)
1 28 ounce can plum tomatoes (torn in bite size pieces)
1 clove garlic (minced)
1/4 cup dry white wine
1/4 cup olive oil
1 tablespoon parsley
1 teaspoon salt
1/4 teaspoon pepper

In a large skillet, heat olive oil over medium heat. Season porkchops with salt, pepper and parsley. Fry until browned on both sides. Remove from pan. Add garlic, mushrooms and peppers. Saute for 10 minutes. Slowly stir in tomatoes with all the juice and wine. Return porkchops to pan. Cover and cook at a low simmer for about 1 hour or until tender.

On Valentine's Day, one of the most popular gifts to give a partner is 'Baci Perugina'. These are small chocolate covered hazelnuts, that are similar to fortune cookies, in that they contain a small piece of paper, however these slips of paper contain only romantic poetic quotes

BRACIUOLINI

1 pound flank steak (sliced very thin)
1/2 cup olive oil
3 tablespoons olive oil
1 clove garlic
2 tablespoons parsley
3 tablespoons Parmesan cheese
1/8 teaspoon salt
1/8 teaspoon pepper
Kitchen twine

This fork tender meat roll is to be made to add to a Marinara sauce. In a large skillet, heat 1/2 cup olive oil over medium heat. Spread a thin layer of olive oil over each slice of meat. In a bowl, mix garlic, parsley, cheese and salt and pepper. Spread about 1 1/2 teaspoons of this mixture over the oiled side of the meat. Roll each piece of meat carefully into a log-like shape. Fasten both ends and the middle of the meat with kitchen twine. Place in the skillet and brown on both sides (about 5 minutes). Remove from pan and add to tomato sauce. This should cook in sauce for approximately 2-3 hours. This wonderful piece of meat will be bursting with flavor and will absolutely melt in your mouth upon serving.

MARINATED PORK TENDERLOIN

3 pound Pork Tenderloin
10 small red potatoes (cut in half)
3 cloves garlic (minced)
5 large basil leaves (cut in half)
3 oregano sprigs
1 teaspoon salt
1/2 teaspoon pepper
1/4 cup balsamic vinegar
1 1/2 cups olive oil

Place Pork Tenderloin and all above ingredients (except potatoes) in a large freezer bag. Refrigerate at least 6 hours, turning bag periodically , to marinate throughout. Place Tenderloin in a large

baking dish and pour all juices over the top. Place potatoes around pork and drizzle a little more olive oil over the top. Bake at 325 degrees for approximately 1 1/2 hours. For more accuracy, use a meat thermometer that will read 160 degrees for readiness. Once done, remove from oven and cover with aluminum foil for about 20 minutes, since it will be much easier to cut.

> Traditionally, Italians choose names for their children from the name of a grandparent, choosing names from the father's side of the family first and then from the mother's side. At other times, children are named after a Saint on whose Feast Day they were born, or with one whom the parents feel a special connection

Contorni

While the second course of the
Italian meal primarily consists of
a meat or fish entree, there are
also many vegetables, rices and
salads to serve as well. To
accompany a main course, there
are countless numbers of side
dishes to choose from, that can
help to compliment your meal.
The following are many of the
popular selections that Italians
love most

Wines to Serve with Contorni

Since vegetables are rarely the main course, wines are usually matched with the meat, fish or poultry dish they are served with. Those vegetable dishes that are served alone usually call for a wine on the light side, such as a dry white wine, like a Sauvignon Blanc. For those tomato based heavier vegetable dishes (like an eggplant parmesan), a light red like a Barbera or medium-bodied red like a Merlot are well suited. If serving mushrooms, a well aged, strong red wine, like an aged Chianti is great. There are some vegetable dishes, such as asparagus, spinach, artichokes and ones that are made with a lot of lemon or vinegar that are not well suited with wine at all.

STUFFED EGGPLANT

3 large eggplant
3 cloves garlic (minced)
1/2 cup olive oil
1/2 pound lean ground beef
1/2 pound sweet Italian sausage
1 large ripe tomato
1 cup Mozzarella cheese
2 cups Marinara sauce

Cut eggplant longways down the center, so you have two large halves. Cut out the middle of the eggplant, so just the shell remains. Place shells in a large baking dish. Preheat oven to 350 degrees. Dice the pulp of the eggplant and set aside. In a large skillet, heat 1/2 cup of olive oil on medium heat. Add eggplant and saute for 7 minutes. Remove eggplant from the pan and set aside. Add the remaining oil, along with the garlic, ground beef and sausage, breaking the meats up into small pieces. Continue to saute until well browned. Add eggplant and tomato sauce to pan. Simmer for an additional 5 minutes. Remove from heat. Place 1/4-1/2 cup of meat mixture into each of the eggplant shells, depending on their size. Slice tomato into circles, and place one tomato slice and some Mozzarella cheese on each piece of eggplant. Bake for 40 minutes. Serve immediately.

RATATOUILLE

1 large yellow squash (scraped & cubed)
1 large zucchini (scraped & cubed)
1 small eggplant (peeled & cubed)
1 medium onion (sliced longways)
2 cloves garlic (minced)
1 28 ounce can plum tomatoes (torn into large bite size pieces)
1/2 cup olive oil
1 teaspoon oregano

1 teaspoon basil
1/2 teaspoon salt
1/4 teaspoon pepper

In a large skillet heat oil over medium heat. Add all vegetables except tomatoes and saute for about 12 minutes. Add tomatoes with all juice and seasonings and saute for an additional 15 minutes. Serve with Romano cheese.

Bocce is probably one of the most popular sports enjoyed by Italians. It consists of 8 large balls a 1 small ball called a 'pallino'. There are two teams, with varying numbers of players and the object is simple. As you throw the balls across the lawn, you hope to get your four bocce balls as close to the pallino as possible. You are allowed to knock opponents balls out of the way, which is actually quite a fun part of the game. You get a point for each round you win, and play up until what ever number chosen

PONZINOITTES (POTATO PATTIES)

8 white potatoes
1/2 cup Italian seasoned bread crumbs
1/2 cup olive oil
1 cup Parmesan cheese
2 eggs
1 tablespoon butter
1 teaspoon salt
1/2 teaspoon pepper

In a large pot bring 3 quarts of water to a aboil. Add potatoes and boil until firm (about 20 minutes). Remove from water and allow

to cool. Peel skins off potatoes and discard. Place potatoes in a large bowl. Add cheese, eggs, butter, salt and pepper. Mash potatoes well. Cover bowl and place in refrigerator. Allow to firm about 1 1/2 hours. In a large skillet, heat olive oil over medium/high heat. Roll potatoes into small logs about 1 inch wide and 3 inches long. Place bread crumbs in a small bowl, and roll potato logs into them. Fry until browned on all sides. Serve hot.

How to Peel a Tomato

Ever wonder if there was an easier way to peel a tomato, without removing some of that precious pulp? Well there is. Just bring a pot of water to a boil, and blanche tomatoes in water about 30 seconds. When you remove them, the skin will probably already be peeling, so just continue to remove the remainder of the skin.

STUFFED ARTICHOKES

6 large artichokes
1/2 16 ounce can black olives (chopped)
1 cup buttered crackers (crushed to a fine texture)
1/4 cup Parmesan cheese
1 clove garlic (minced)
1/4 cup olive oil
1 tablespoon parsley
1/2 teaspoon salt
1/8 teaspoon pepper
1/2 cup chicken broth
4 tablespoons butter

Wash artichokes, and cut off tips on the top. Cut off stems, and set aside. The artichokes should be able to stand upright. Tap the tops of artichokes lightly on a cutting board to spread leaves slightly open. In a medium size mixing bowl, mix all above ingredients to make stuffing. Dice stems and add to stuffing mixture. Add 1/4 cup of water to stuffing to help make it cling. Place stuffing in artichokes until it is all used up. Place artichokes in a large pan and add 4 cups of water, chicken broth and butter, so the liquid is just about half way up the sides of the artichokes. Drizzle a little more olive oil over the top. Bring water in the pan to a boil, then reduce heat to a simmer, cover and cook for approximately 1 hour or until leaves are tender. Season with salt.

EGGPLANT ROLATINE

2 eggplant
1 pound 100% skim milk Ricotta cheese
5 eggs
1/4 cup milk
2 cups flour
1 cup olive oil
2 teaspoons parsley
1/4 teaspoon pepper
1 12 ounce package Mozzarella cheese
3 cups Marinara sauce

Peel and slice eggplant into 1/4 inch rounds. Layer eggplant in a strainer and lightly salt each layer, cover, and allow to sit about 1 hour. Once hour is up, drain excess liquid that accumulates from eggplant and pat dry on towel paper. In a large skillet, heat olive oil on medium heat. In a small bowl, beat 3 eggs and season with a little salt and pepper. In another bowl, place flour. Dip each eggplant slice in egg, then in flour. Fry until golden brown on both sides. Remove from pan and drain on paper towel to remove excess oil. Next, in a large bowl, mix Ricotta cheese, milk, 2 eggs, parsley, pepper and 1/2 package of Mozzarella cheese. Blend well. Place 1 tablespoon of mixture in center of each eggplant and roll to close. In a large baking dish, place 1 cup Marinara sauce, and spread. Place each eggplant "seam" down on sauce. Add more sauce, the rest of the Mozzarella and Parmesan cheese on top. Cover and bake at 350 degrees for 45 minutes.

ITALIAN VEGETABLE CASSEROLE

1 medium eggplant (peeled & sliced into 1/2" rounds)
2 green peppers (sliced)
2 red peppers (sliced)
4 potatoes (peeled & sliced into 1/2" rounds)
3 cloves garlic (chopped)
1 pound plum tomatoes (peeled & diced)
1/2 cup olive oil
1 teaspoon salt
1/2 teaspoon pepper

In a medium skillet, heat 1/4 cup of the olive oil on medium heat. Fry eggplant and potatoes, turning continuously for about 10 minutes. In another frying pan, warm remaining olive oil on

medium heat and saute peppers until tender. In a large casserole dish, layer potatoes, then peppers, then eggplant. Add 2 cloves of garlic and then tomatoes. Sprinkle with salt and pepper. Bake at 350 degrees for 35 minutes. Serve with freshly grated Romano cheese.

My grandmother always would use fresh mushrooms from her backyard. According to an old wives tale, to tell if the mushrooms were poisonous, she would put a new shiny penny in boiling water with the mushrooms, and if the copper of the penny turned a dark color, they were not to be eaten. She swore by this method, and everyone who ate her mushrooms are still around to talk about it....

Popular Italian Vocabulary

Even if you are not from the "old country" , there is countless lingo used in Italian households and throughout our society. Here are some of the most popular:

Paisani: (pronounced Pisan) The name given for a fellow Italian
Salute: Cheers!; Good health to all
Statti Zitto: (pronounced "sta ta zeet") Shut your mouth
Mappina: Commonly used name for a dish towel
Mangia!Mangia!: Famous words of Italian mothers and
    grandmothers....Eat!Eat!

Vino: Wine

Buon Natale: Merry Christmas

Acida: Heart burn or a stomach ache

Buona Fortuna: Good luck

Madoon: Oh my God!

Grazie: Thank you very much

Baccala: dried salt cod, served many times on Christmas Eve

Stonato: (pronounced stunod) a dummy or a dingbat

Tarantella: A traditional Italian dance, done many times at weddings or other festive occasions

Buon Giorno: Good Morning

La Famiglia: the family

Amore: Love

Capisci: (pronounced Capish) Do you understand?

Goomba: 'Godfather'; someone close, but not a relative

Ciao: Hello & Goodbye

ZUCCHINI CASSEROLE

4 large zucchini
1 large yellow onion
1/2 cup olive oil
4 tablespoons butter
1 12 ounce package of Monterey Jack cheese
1/2 cup plain bread crumbs
Salt & pepper to taste

Scrape the peel of each zucchini, so there is still some peel remaining and rinse well. Slice each zucchini into 1/4 inch

rounds. Slice onion into rounds as thin as possible. In a large casserole dish, layer half of the zucchini slices, half of the onion slices, 1/2 package of Monterey Jack cheese, then 1/4 cup of olive oil. Then layer the remainder of the zucchini, onion, cheese and oil in the same order. Sprinkle some salt and pepper, then top with bread crumbs, covering all the cheese. Place small pats of butter throughout the top to help brown the bread crumbs. Bake uncovered on 400 degrees for 45 minutes.

> *To an Italian, gossip is second only to religion in order of importance. For Italians, the better the gossip, the longer the talks, the more time to spend together with friends*

SICILIAN GREEN BEANS

1 pound green beans
1/4 cup bread crumbs
1/4 cup Parmesan cheese
1/4 cup sliced almonds
1 clove garlic (minced)
2 tablespoons butter

In a medium pan, bring 5 cups water to a boil. Cook green beans

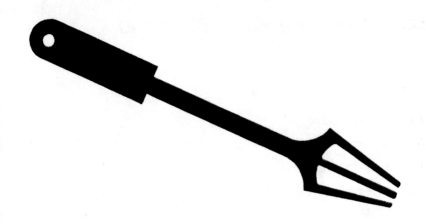

until tender, about 12 minutes, and set aside. In a medium skillet, heat butter on low heat. Saute garlic for 3 minutes. Add almonds and bread crumbs and toast lightly. Add to cooked string beans. Toss well. Add Parmesan cheese and serve hot.

Do you ever wonder why Italians are so loud? Italian family life can often be, to an outsider an array of noise and commotion. Being raised around Italians my entire life, this was a foreign idea until my non-Italian brother-in-law entered our family. He found it amazing that although there would be 10 people at the dinner table, it would sound like there's 30. He has pointed out to us on numerous occasions, and continues to, that at our table there are usually many conversations going on at once, and can't believe how each person is usually able to carry on a conversation and still hear and add their opinion to another conversation, then go right back to their previous conversation. I guess this talent is learned early on, if one wants to be heard at all.....

CARCIOFI FRITTI (FRIED ARTICHOKES)

1 16 ounce can artichoke hearts (not marinated)
2 eggs
2 tablespoons olive oil
1/2 teaspoon salt
1 teaspoon garlic powder
1/2 cup lemon juice
3/4 cup flour
2/3 cup lukewarm water
1/4 cup olive oil

In a medium bowl, combine eggs, 2 tablespoons oil, salt, flour, garlic powder and water. Set aside for about 1 hour. Slice artichokes into quartered pieces. In a small bowl, combine artichokes and lemon juice, and soak for 30 minutes. In a skillet warm olive oil on high heat. Drain artichokes on paper towel. Dip artichokes in batter and fry until golden brown. Serve with a dash of lemon and Ranch dressing if desired.

In the beginning of this century, many Italian men traveled to America looking for a new start in life, and once settled, would send for their families back in Italy. During this time, these men longed for the customs and traditions of home, and would reproduce them by forming an extended family with other Italians, where they could get that sense of togetherness and companionship, most often through food, drink and conversation

MARINATED MUSHROOMS

5 12 ounce packages whole white mushrooms (washed well)
1/4 cup olive oil
1 1/2 cups white wine vinegar
3 cloves garlic (minced)
1/4 cup lemon juice
1/8 teaspoon rosemary
1 bay leaf
1/8 teaspoon salt
1/8 teaspoon pepper
1 Mason jar

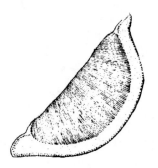

In a medium sauce pan bring 1/2 gallon of salted water to a boil. Throw in mushrooms and cook for about 10 minutes or until tender. Remove mushrooms and let them air dry. In a large skillet, warm olive oil over medium heat. Place mushrooms in pan, and saute for 5 minutes. Remove from pan, and place in a large mixing bowl. Add garlic to pan and allow to saute until soft. Add garlic and oil to mushrooms and blend well. Stir in vinegar and remainder of seasonings until well mixed. Place in a jar and refrigerate. Tastes best if made a few days in advance.

> Traditionally at Italian weddings, women are given candy-coated almonds (known as bomboniera), wrapped in tulle. There are usually 5 or 7 (both lucky numbers) candies per package. And men are traditionally given cigars.

EGGPLANT PARMESAN

1 large eggplant
1 cup flour
3 eggs
1 cup olive oil
1 12 ounce package Mozzarella cheese
1/2 cup Parmesan cheese
1 teaspoon salt
1/2 teaspoon pepper

Peel and slice eggplant into 1/4 inch rounds. Layer eggplant in a strainer and lightly salt each layer. Put a dish on top and allow to sit for about 1 hour. Drain excess liquid from eggplant and pat dry on towel paper. In a large skillet, warm olive oil over medium heat. In a small bowl, place flour with salt and pepper. In another bowl beat eggs well. Dip each slice of eggplant into eggs, then

flour. Place in hot oil and fry until golden brown on both sides (about 5 minutes). Place on paper towel to drain excess oil. In a large baking dish, ladle some sauce onto the bottom. Place a layer of eggplant, some more sauce, then sprinkle some Mozzarella cheese, then some Parmesan cheese. Put some more sauce, and continue layering until all of the eggplant is used. The top layer should be some sauce with a little Mozzarella to melt. Bake at 350 degrees for 30 minutes. Great as a side dish to a tomato based pasta dish, or just served with a loaf of crusty Italian bread.

ITALIAN PASTA SALAD

1 pound tri-colored rotini pasta
1 red pepper (cleaned & diced)
1 green pepper (cleaned & diced)
1 16 ounce can black olives (chopped)
1/2 cup cubed Mozzarella cheese
1 package Good Seasons Dressing (using red wine vinegar)

In a large pan, bring 3 quarts water to a boil. Cook pasta according to box directions. Drain and place in a large bowl. Add peppers and olives and mix well. Add half of Good Seasons Dressing, and allow to chill in refrigerator. When ready to serve, add Mozzarella cheese and remainder of dressing, and mix well.

"La Dolce Vita", meaning "The Sweet Life" is truly how Italians view their lifestyle. In Italy, life is characterized by simplicity, where most don't seem to have a care in the world. The pace of life is much more relaxed, where individuals take the time to enjoy talking, interacting and sharing the company of others as a main priority. For an Italian, as long as you have family, friends and something good to eat... life is good

BROCCOLI RABE WITH GARLIC

1 large bunch broccoli rabe
3 cloves garlic (sliced thin)
3 cups water
2 cups chicken broth
1/2 cup olive oil
1 teaspoon salt
1/4 teaspoon pepper
1/4 Romano cheese

Wash brocolli rabe well. In a deep skillet, add broccoli rabe, water and chicken broth, and bring to a boil. Cook for about 12 minutes or until stems feel tender. Once cooked, drain and set aside. Reduce heat to low/medium, and add oil and garlic to the pan. Saute for about 4 minutes. Return broccoli rabe to pan, add salt and pepper and continue to saute for about 10 more minutes. Sprinkle with Romano cheese.

Italians, just like many other cultures, have their share of superstitions. One of the more popular superstitions, is for Italians to protect themselves from "mal'occhio", or "the evil eye". Many Italians wear two types of charms for this purpose. The first is the Italian horn, which is said to protect one from the evil eye, and the other is the closed hand with index and pinky fingers pointed which is said to ward off the evil eye, and if pointed toward someone who wishes you ill will, it will go right back to them, therefore protecting oneself

ITALIAN GRILLED VEGETABLES

1 eggplant (peeled & sliced longways in large strips)
2 squash (peeled & sliced longways)
1 zucchini (peeled & sliced)
1 large red onion (sliced in circles)
3 large portabello mushrooms (cut in half)
1 red pepper (cut into wedges)
4 cloves garlic (minced)

1/4 cup olive oil
3 tablespoons balsamic vinegar
1 tablespoon parsley
1 teaspoon basil
1 teaspoon salt
1/4 teaspoon pepper

Combine all above ingredients in a large mixing bowl. Cover tightly and marinate in the refrigerator for about 2 hours, stirring mixture twice throughout. Prepare grill. Remove vegetables from bag, and place on grill rack that is coated with cooking spray. Pour the remainder of dressing over vegetables. Grill about 12 minutes, turning occasionally. Great served with grilled chicken and a loaf of crusty Italian bread.

Many Italians use Sunday as the day to get together with family. "Sunday dinner" as it is appropriately called usually would be eaten mid-day, and consist of pasta, meatballs, sausage, bread and salads.

PORTABELLO MUSHROOMS

4 large portabello mushrooms
2 cloves garlic (minced)
1/4 cup olive oil
1/4 cup Marsala wine
Salt & Pepper to taste

In a large skillet, warm olive oil on medium heat. To clean portabello mushrooms, wipe well with paper towel and do not rinse, since they will get a slimy film on them. Add mushrooms to

pan and saute for 10 minutes, turning occasionally. Add garlic and saute another 4 minutes. Add Marsala wine and allow to cook an additional 5 minutes for wine to cook down. Serve as a side dish, or on Italian bread with some roasted peppers on top. Season with salt and pepper.

In Italian tradition, fava beans are considered a source of good luck. During a time in Italian history when all other crops failed, the fava beans continued to grow in great abundance. It then became known as a lucky bean, and whomever carried a blessed bean in their purse or pocket, they would never be without coins or would never go hungry

SQUASH FLOWER PATTIES

30 squash flowers
1 egg
1 cup flour
3/4 cup cream
3 tablespoons grated Parmesan cheese
1 teaspoon baking soda
1 teaspoon Italian seasoning
1/2 teaspoon garlic powder
1/4 teaspoon salt
1/8 teaspoon pepper
1 cup olive oil
Salt to taste

Rinse squash flowers well and pat dry. Place all above ingredients except squash flowers, flour and oil into a medium bowl and mix well. You will then add flour gradually, stirring to avoid clumping. In a large skillet, heat olive oil on medium/high heat. Take squash flowers and dip them one at a time into batter, then place in hot oil. It should immediately start sizzling. Fry on each side, about 2 minutes or until golden brown. Drain on paper towel. Serve hot. *Not many stores sell these, so this dish may be for those who are growing squash in their own garden and wonder what they can do with those wonderful yellow flowers that appear on their squash plants!

BEAN SALAD

1 pound bow tie pasta
1 stalk celery (diced)
2 ripe tomatoes (diced)
1 clove garlic (minced)
1 15 ounce can chick peas (drained & rinsed)
1 15 ounce can red kidney beans (drained & rinsed)
1 15 ounce can Cannellini beans (drained & rinsed)
1 6 ounce jar roasted peppers (sliced very thin)
1/2 cup olive oil
1/4 cup red wine vinegar
1 teaspoon Italian seasoning
1/2 teaspoon salt
1/4 teaspoon pepper
1/4 cup Parmesan cheese

In a medium pan, bring 3 quarts of water to a boil. Cook pasta according to box directions. Drain and rinse with cold water. Add celery, tomatoes, garlic, chick peas, kidney &cannellini beans and roasted peppers and mix well. Add 1/4 cup of olive oil and stir to avoid pasta from sticking. Allow to chill in refrigerator. When ready to serve, add remainder of oil, vinegar, Italian seasoning, salt, pepper and Parmesan cheese. A refreshing summer treat!

MUSHROOM RISOTTO

1 12 ounce package white mushrooms (sliced)
2 large portabello mushrooms (sliced)
2 cloves garlic (minced)
1 leek (diced; white part only)
1 1/2 cups water
1 1/2 cups chicken broth
1/4 cup dry sherry

2 tablespoons butter
2 tablespoons olive oil
1/2 cup Parmesan cheese
1 teaspoon thyme
1/2 teaspoon salt
1/4 teaspoon pepper
1 pound Arborio rice

In a medium saucepan bring water and broth to a boil. Add rice
and cook according to box directions. Drain and save excess
liquid. In a a large skillet, heat oil and butter over medium heat.
Add garlic and leek and saute approximately 3 minutes. Add
mushrooms and cook for about 5 minutes or until they begin to
soften. Reduce heat to low, cover and cook an additional 5
minutes. Add seasonings, sherry and 1/2 cup of reserved liquid.
Stir uncovered for 5 minutes. Add rice, stirring continuously to
avoid sticking, and continue cooking until almost all of the liquid
is absorbed. Remove from heat, stir in Parmesan cheese and serve

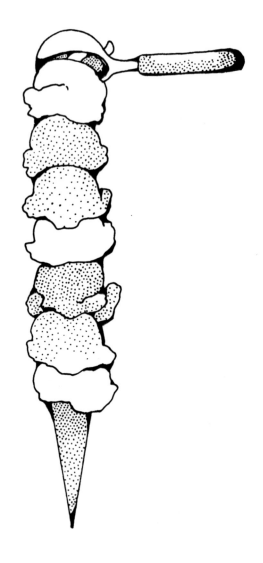

Dolci

An Italian meal is typically
followed by a variety of fresh
fruits and cheeses, or fruit based
desserts. However, Italians still
tend to have a sweet tooth. And
on holidays or other special
occassions and celebrations,
Italians enjoy indulging in rich
desserts and a glass of sweet
wine or Italian coffee

Wines to Serve with Dolci

Desserts and fruits are best complimented by sweet and sparkling wines. For lightly sweetened desserts, such as Biscotti or pastries, bubbly, crisp wines like Asti Spumante or Moscato d'asti are best. When serving richer desserts like cheesecake or Tiramisu, sweeter wines like Maslvasia or Ice Wine are great. And when serving fruit or fruit based desserts, Prosecco is a wonderful choice. Some desserts, such as plain chocolate, pudding or ice cream, should not be served with wine.

AMARETTO FRUIT DIP

1 8 ounce package cream cheese (cut in chunks)
1/2 cup confectioners sugar
4 tablespoons Amaretto liquor
Assortment fruit (strawberries, peaches, kiwi, honeydew melon,
                    cantaloupe)

In a food processor, blend cream cheese and Amaretto well. Add
sugar and continue processing until smooth. Place in a decorative
dip bowl, surrounded by various fruit.

WINE MARINATED PEACHES

6 large ripe peaches (peeled & sliced into thin wedges)
1 orange
Juice from 1/2 lemon
2 tablespoons confectioners sugar
1 cup Sweet or Sparkling white wine (Chill and save rest of wine)

Place peach wedges into a bowl. Cut lemon in half and squeeze
juice over peaches. Peel orange and grind about 1 tablespoon of
peel and add to peaches. Squeeze juice from remaining orange
over peaches. Pour wine over peaches and cover. Refrigerate for
at least 6 hours. Either place some peaches in a wine glass with
some of the remaining wine or on a plate with a scoop of vanilla
ice cream.

The Low Down on Cheese

There are many different types of cheeses used in Italian cooking and in the household. For Italians, no day is complete without eating cheese in one tasty form or another. Some of the most popular ones are:

ASIAGO: a hard cheese consisting of a fruity slightly sharp taste. This cheese has intense flavor, due to its long slow maturation process of over 2 years. It is usually used grated and as a condiment.

FONTINA: a dense smooth cheese with a delicate nuttiness and a hint of mild honey. When melted, as it frequently isthe flavor is earthy with a taste of mushrooms. It is also great as a table and dessert cheese

FRESH MOZZARELLA: a fresh soft cheese, which is generally mild, and high in moisture, and therefore low in fat. It can at times be slightly acidic. It is mostly used in cooking, but it is also served as a table cheese with fresh herbs and marinated or fresh vegetables

GORGONZOLA: both a mild and sharp cheese, which is great in salads and in dips

PROVOLONE: a semi-hard cheese that is supple and smooth, and generally considered an all-purpose cheese. It can be used for cooking, as a topping for sandwiches as well as for dessert purposes and even grating. It can also be used as a table cheese

PARMESAN : a hard cheese with a wonderful sweet fruity taste and aroma. This is primarily a grating cheese, and is a great topping for soups, pasta dishes and salads.....or anything else for that matter

ROMANO: a hard cheese, with a sharp flavor. It is one of Italy's oldest cheeses and is generally used for grating

RICOTTA: a soft cheese that is white creamy and mild. It is a basin shaped cheese, pure white and wet, but not sticky. The most popular use of this cheese is as an ingredient in lasagna or as a stuffing in other sauce-based dishes

ITALIAN TORTE

6 large red delicious apples
1/2 lemon rind (grated)
12 Macaroon cookies (crushed)
1/4 cup sugar
4 eggs (slightly beaten)
2 tablespoons flour
1/2 teaspoon nutmeg
1/4 teaspoon almond extract
1/4 cup milk
Almonds/Maraschino cherries to garnish

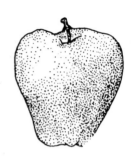

Peel and grate apples, and place in a large mixing bowl. Add
lemon rind, Macaroon crumbs, sugar, salt, flour, nutmeg, eggs
and almond extract. Mix together thoroughly. Stir in milk and
blend well. Pout into a well greased 8 inch baking dish. Dot top
with butter and bake in a slow oven on 300-325 degrees for 2
hours. Decorate with blanched almonds and Maraschino cherries.
Chill before serving, plain or with whipped cream.

Italians don't just communicate through talking. A
popular trait among Italians is the movement of
hands while talking. It seems as though they just
can't help it. I have amusingly asked my mother
many times to just try and not move her hands while
talking, and it appears to be a form of medieval
torture for her

ANGINETTES

6 eggs
1 cup vegetable oil
1 cup sugar
1 cup orange juice
5 teaspoons baking powder
1 teaspoon baking soda
1/2 teaspoon vanilla extract
1/2 teaspoon lemon extract
speck of salt
5 1/2 cups flour
Frosting:
2 cups confectioners sugar
drop of vanilla extract
2 tablespoons water
colored ball sprinkles

In a large bowl, mix oil and sugar, then add eggs, orange juice, salt, vanilla and lemon extract. Mix well. Add baking powder and soda, stir thoroughly. Add flour gradually, and add just as much as it takes to make dough soft and pliable (usually a little more than 5 cups). Knead dough on a floured board for 5 minutes. Make into 1/2" balls, and place on a cookie sheet. Bake at 375 degrees for 10 minutes. Allow to cool. Meanwhile, mix all frosting ingredients together well (add more water if too thick for your liking). Once cool, dip top of cookies in mixture, then shake on some sprinkles and set on wax paper. Allow to sit for one hour.

GENOVESE (THE CAKE OF GENOA)

Cake:
5 eggs
1 cup sugar
1 teaspoon vanilla
1/2 teaspoon salt
1 1/4 cup flour

Cream filling:
3/4 cup sugar
2 tablespoons cornstarch
6 egg yolks
1 1/2 cups milk

Chocolate icing:
2 tablespoons butter (softened)
1 cup confectioners sugar
1 egg
1 ounce melted chocolate

1 teaspoon vanilla   *1/2 teaspoon vanilla*

1/2 cup softened butter

In a large bowl, beat eggs until light and fluffy. Gradually add sugar, vanilla and salt, and continue to blend. Add flour slowly, and fold into mixture thoroughly. Grease 2 8 inch round layer pans. Add batter. Bake at 350 degrees for 25-30 minutes. Allow to cool. Remove cake when cooled and cut in half to make 4 round cakes. To make cream filling, in a pan, combine sugar and cornstarch and warm over medium heat. Add yolks and milk stirring continuously, until thickened. Remove from heat and add vanilla. Cool and blend in butter. Spread cream filling between layers and on sides of cake. In a medium bowl, combine all ingredients of chocolate icing and beat until smooth. Frost top of cake with icing.

PIGNOLI COOKIES

1 pound almond paste
2 cups granulated sugar
1/4 cup flour
4 egg whites
1/2 pound Pignoli nuts (chopped)

Mix all above ingredients (except Pignoli nuts) and stir thoroughly.
Dough will be sticky. Put flour on hands and take about 1
tablespoon of dough at a time, and roll into nuts. Place on a greased
cookie sheet and bake at 275 degrees for 17 minutes.

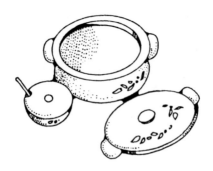

AMBROSIA

1 large pineapple (cut into chunks)
2 11 ounce cans mandarin oranges
2 cups mini marshmallows
2 cups flaked coconut
2 cups sour cream
1 tablespoon brown sugar
1 jar maraschino cherries

Drain mandarin oranges. In a large bowl, combine pineapple,
oranges, marshmallows, coconut and brown sugar. Mix well.
Combine with sour cream and stir. Place in a glass bowl, so all
colors can be seen . Top with cheeries and refrigerate until serving.

TIRAMISU

1 cup black coffee (cooled)
36 lady finger cookies
8 ounces Mascarpone cheese (softened)
1 1/4 cups whipping cream
1 teaspoon vanilla extract
1 tablespoon confectioners sugar
1/2 cup of sweetened chocolate (chopped)
1/4 cup condensed milk
6 tablespoons brandy
Cinnamon to garnish

Cut lady fingers in half. In a medium bowl, mix black coffee with brandy. Take lady fingers and brush coffee mixture generously (not to soak) on both sides. Set aside on wax paper. In a large bowl, combine cheese, whipping cream, 1/4 cup of the black coffee mixture, confectioners sugar and vanilla. Gradually beat this mixture until soft peaks form. In a small saucepan, melt the chocolate with 1/4 cup condensed milk. In large dessert glasses, layer Mascarpone mixture, melted chocolate, lady fingers, then the Mascarpone mixture ending on the top. This should make about 8 desserts. Cover and chill about 5 hours. Serve with whipped cream on top if desired. Sprinkle top with powdered cinnamon.

ITALIAN CREAM PIE

Crust:
3 cups flour
1/2 cup sugar
5 heaping tablespoons vegetable shortening
3 teaspoons baking powder
1 1/2 teaspoons vanilla
4 eggs
Filling:
6 egg yolks
1 cup sugar
4 tablespoons flour
4 cups milk
3/4 teaspoon vanilla
1 cup sweetened chocolate (chopped)
1/2 teaspoon salt
1 egg (slightly beaten)

In a large bowl, add all crust ingredients. Knead and roll out to a thin dough. Be sure that the dough is rolled out enough to cover the bottom and top of a pastry dish. In a medium bowl, beat 6 egg yolks, sugar, flour and salt. Beat for about 5 minutes. Place this mixture in a medium saucepan and heat on low. Add milk 1 cup at a time, stirring throughout. Continue to stir until mixture has thickened. Add vanilla and chocolate. Stir until chocolate has melted. Remove from heat. Cut dough in half, and place in bottom

ITALIAN CREAM PIE (con't)

of pastry dish (some dough should be hanging over the sides). Pour cream mixture into shell. Cover with remainder of dough. Pinch edges with fork so it seals, and trim any remaining dough. Rub top of the crust with beaten egg yolk. Cook for 30 minutes on 350 degrees. Cool, then refrigerate. When ready to serve, sift with confectioners sugar.

ITALIAN FRUIT COOKIES

4 cups flour
4 tablespoons shortening
4 teaspoons baking powder
4 eggs
2 cups sugar
1/4 pound dried mixed fruit
1/4 pound sweetened chocolate (chopped)
1/4 pound raisins
1/4 teaspoon cinnamon

Wash raisins with warm water and sprinkle with cinnamon. In a large bowl, combine flour, shortening, baking powder, sugar, fruit, chocolate and raisins. Mix well. In a small bowl, slightly beat eggs and add to mixture. Place mixture in a well greased 9x13 pan and bake at 350 degrees for 20 minutes. Allow to cool and cut into long log cookies. Put on baking sheet and cook another 7 minutes.

Starting Your Own Wine Cellar

There are many benefits to creating and starting a wine cellar in your very own home. Not only would you always have a specific bottle that you like on hand, you will always have a selection of wines available. Also, you will have the ability to buy and store fine wines that will improve in taste and value as they mature. You would be able to buy these fine wines when they are young and least expensive and be able to put them away to mature properly, so you can enjoy them at a later time.

When starting to create a wine cellar, you will want to be sure to shop at a liquor store with a knowledgeable wine salesperson. This person can not only help in choosing the best wines to store and

buy, they should be able to possibly introduce you to new vintages or let you know when a great wine will be coming in.

Many times, individuals are unsure if they have the space in their home to start a wine cellar. However, if you have an empty corner in a basement or a free closet, you're on your way to getting started. Wherever you decide to create your wine cellar, you must be sure that it is a dark place where the wine can remain undisturbed, and that the area is relatively cool. If the wine is stored in a warm atmosphere, the taste will eventually be dull, flat or vinegary, and it will age much more rapidly. In this area you should have a wooden wine rack (they're sturdiest), where bottles could be stored on their sides to keep the corks moist.

When one starts a wine cellar, the lingering question is always "Well now when can I drink this wine?". Most wines, especially whites are ready to drink when you buy them, and do not require prolonged aging. Sauvignon Blanc, Pinot Grigio, Chardoney, Roses', Sparkling and Sweet wines are best when they're fresh and young and rarely improve with age. More concentrated reds, like Chiantis are better at 4 or 5 years of age. Cabernet Sauvignon and Merlots need about 6-8 years to age for the best taste.

A wine cellar should have about a years' worth supply of wine for current drinking. When stocking your wine cellar you should cover

basic dining needs and a selection for a range of tastes. But be sure to never buy in quantity before trying a bottle. For a safe bet, you will want 1 case of the following wines, and maybe 2 of the ones you consume more often.

Sparkling Wine (appetizers/desserts)

Sauvignon Blanc or Pinot Grigio (fish/chicken/salad/pastas)

Chardoney (fish/chicken/pork/appetizers)

Roses' or Blushes (salads/light dishes)

Cabernet Sauvignon (beef/roasts/strong cheeses)

Merlot (pasta/veal)

Chianti (beef/veal/pasta/mushrooms)

Be sure to seperate wines into ones that need aging and ones that don't. But most importantly, be sure to vary the wines according to your own needs and preferences, as well as those you may need for entertaining.

LEMON MASCARPONE CHEESECAKE

Crust:
1 1/2 cups graham cracker crumbs (crushed to a fine texture)
3 tablespoons sugar
1/2 teaspoon cinnamon
4 tablespoons butter (melted)
Filling:
1 1/2 pounds Mascarpone cheese
2 lemons
1 cup sugar
2 large eggs (separated)
1/2 teaspoon vanilla

In a large bowl, combine cracker crumbs, sugar, cinnamon and melted butter. Mix well. Grease the bottom and sides of a 10" springform pan. Line the pan with this mixture, going about half way up the pan. Be sure to press tightly together. Peel lemons and grate one lemon peel to a very fine texture. In a medium bowl, beat together cheese, lemon rind, all juice from both lemons, sugar, egg yolks and vanilla until smooth. In a small bowl, beat egg whites

until they are stiff and fold into the cheese mixture. Stir well. Pour mixture into spring pan. Bake at 350 degrees for 40 minutes. Allow cheesecake to cool before removing from pan. Be sure to refrigerate before serving.

ZEPPOLE

1 pound Ricotta cheese
5 eggs
1 tablespoon vanilla
1/2 cup sugar
2 cups flour
4 teaspoons baking powder
1 cup olive oil
Pinch of salt

In a large bowl, beat eggs well. Add vanilla and Ricotta cheese and mix. Next add sugar and baking powder, continuing to stir well. Finally add flour and mix until well blended. In a large skillet, heat olive oil over medium/high heat. Spoon about 1 tablespoon of dough into oil, and cook until golden brown, turning once during cooking time. Allow to cool. Once cool, sprinkle with powdered sugar and serve.

Although many people may be unaware, January 6th (The Epiphany) is a very important celebration for Italians. This day is also known as "Little Christmas" and some Italians exchange small gifts on this day. This is the day the 3 wise men arrived at the manger of Christ bearing gifts, and it officially marks the end of the Christmas season.

ITALIAN RICE PUDDING WITH RICOTTA

1/2 pound of rice
1/2 pound Ricotta cheese
1/2 cup sugar
4 eggs (slightly beaten)
1 teaspoon vanilla
Milk (about 1/2 cup)
Cinnamon

In a large saucepan, bring 1 1/2 quarts of water and rice to a boil. Cook rice until almost cooked, drain and put hot rice in a greased baking dish. In a medium bowl, mix sugar, eggs, ricotta and vanilla. Pour mixture over rice and stir slightly (not blended). Cover top of this mixture with some milk, and sprinkle with cinnamon. Bake at 350 degrees for 25 minutes or until set.

One of the wonderful things about Italians is that they love to show affection. So if you are Italian or around a lot of Italians, you better get used to lots of touches, hugs and kissing. While talking to someone, an Italian may tend to touch the person's shoulder or tap them on the arm; this can be a form of endearment, or a way to make sure that they are being listened to. When greeting someone, or saying goodbye, Italians straight from Italy will give you a kiss on both cheeks, while those raised here in America will greet you with a single peck on the cheek.

LEMON ITALIAN ICE

3 lemons

3/4 cup lemon juice (7 lemons)

1/2 cup sugar

2 cups cold water

1 cup fresh berries (raspberries & blueberries)

12 teaspoons confectioners sugar

2 tablespoons of water

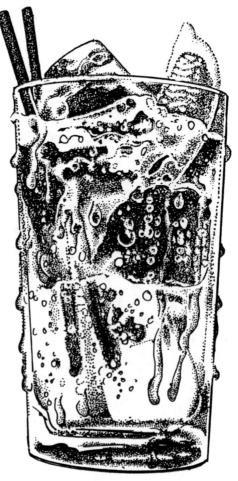

In a small bowl, grate lemon rinds. Add 1/2 cup lemon juice and sugar. Mix well. Place mixture in pan on medium/high heat. Bring to a boil and simmer until thick and syrupy. Pour mixture into large bowl. Add water and the remainder of the lemon juice. Cover and place in the freezer. Freeze for 2 hours. Stir mixture well, breaking up the ice crystals that have formed. Then freeze another hour, until mixture is firm, not solid. Meanwhile, in a small bowl combine berries, confectioners sugar and 2 tablespoons of water and mix. Allow to sit for about 1 hour. Once Italian ice is firm, place scoops into parfait glasses and top with berries.

The most popular Saint in Italy is by far, St. Francis of Assisi, the Patron Saint of all God's creatures. He is said to be the first individual to receive 'the stigmata', which is when someone develops the same wounds on themselves as Christ suffered on the cross, for no apparent reason

<u>*The Italian Grandmother*</u>

Italian grandmothers have been for centuries not only the back bone of the family unit, but the heart and soul as well. "Nonni" as she is affectionately referred to, sees her role as the one to keep the family united and is constantly working on maintaining balance, love and harmony among all family members. It is their only desire that their family will remain close-knit and intact once they are gone, and continue to carry on treasured customs and traditions. Along with their strong family ties and values, Italian grandmothers are notorious for many other special qualities. In

conversations with Italian friends, we would always have a chuckle about the many similarities between our Italian grandmothers. Some things just seem to be innate among them. For instance, why is it that Italian grandmothers feel the need to feed all who enter their home, whether they are hungry or not. There always seemed to be an endless supply of pasta, frasella, biscotti, etc... readily on hand for anyone who comes along. There was always an extra seat (or two) at the family table; and forget about leaving if you came into the home any time a meal was being served. "Just stay and have a little bite to eat", is a famous quote muttered by many an Italian grandmother, with that "little bite to eat", usually being a 5 course meal. Italian grandmothers definitely know how to use food as a way to unite family members and can turn any simple meal into an elaborate occasion. To an Italian grandmother, one of the best ways to show your family how much you love them, is by preparing them a warm, hearty meal.

Italian grandmothers are also well known for humorous, even 'quirky' reasons. For example, once they are up, dressed and ready for the day, why do they feel the need to put on a "moo moo" or "housecoat", which was probably sewn from some extra material laying around. Do they really think this coat compliments them? Well it doesn't really matter, because they would wear it anyway. There is also the empty threat of the wooden spoon.. I could vividly recall watching my barely 5' tall grandmother chasing my cousins with a wooden spoon around the dining room table because they were being a 'malscazone' (rascal). The mere sight of this was hysterical, but the punishment inflicted, if the victim was ever caught was usually just as funny. Grandma just couldn't bring herself to actually use the spoon for more than a slight tap on the bottom - all that running for nothing. But maybe grandma didn't really want to catch them after all. She did, however, have quite an ability to quickly remove her slipper, and send it flying through the air, always nailing her target.

Italian grandmothers are also very tenacious when it comes to their food and preparing meals. You would eat at her house, at the very least, once a week. I can remember my grandmother, without flinching, taking a bucket and some fresh fish, and going out onto her back stoop, with shiny knife in hand. Without a second thought, she would chop off the head, tear out the guts, come back in the house with fish guts all over her apron, and just fry them up. She definitely enjoyed her food, but she always made sure everyone elses plates were full before she would get her own. And even though Italian grandmothers are generally good natured, there is definitely one thing that could set her off. Grandma would defend you like a lioness protecting her cub. So don't bad talk her family, especially her sons or grandchildren, because you'd probably see a side of grandma you'd rather not.

Finally, another popular trait among Italian grandmothers is how they tend to recycle everything and anything. This is said to come from the time of the Great Depression (and also seems to be more true of Southern Italians), when no one really knew when they would have money for certain items, so inevitably they would save things to use for other purposes. They would save Ricotta containers for leftovers and to freeze sauce in, they would save all plastic bags for re-use, they would save bread ties and buttons from shirts for God knows what, they would save old shirts and stockings to tie up tomato plants in the summer, they saved the rinds of lemons and oranges for recipes, they would save old, stale Italian bread to use in stuffing, stews or as bread crumbs, and they would save any and all cards given to them on any occasion, to tear off the front picture, write a note on the back of it and give it to the next person.

Italian grandmothers are definitely one of a kind. Whether it be the delicious food they fill us with, the humorous antics they tend to create, or the extreme warmth and acceptance they provide to their families, one thing is for sure, nothing can replace the love for and the love felt from our Italian grandmothers.

BISCOTTI

1/4 cup butter (softened)
1 cup sugar
2 teaspoons baking powder
4 eggs
1 1/2 cups flour
2 teaspoons vanilla
1/2 cup vegetable oil

Preheat oven to 350 degrees. Lightly grease a cookie sheet with butter. In a large bowl, beat eggs for about 5 minutes. Add remainder of ingredients and mix well. Knead dough and shape into two loaf-like rolls. Place on cookie sheet and flatten somewhat. Bake for 30 minutes, then cut into 1 inch slices. Place slices cut side down on an ungreased cookie sheet, and bake another 10 minutes or until Biscotti are dry and crisp. For a little extra flavor, you can add either a 1/2 cup of sweetened chocolate chopped into pieces, or 1/4 cup of dried mixed fruit to the dough mixture.

Italians are known to love good food, good wine, family and friends. Thinking of Italian based movies, they all have at least one scene of many people sitting around a table, eating, drinking, laughing and enjoying each others conversation

SPUMONE

1 pint vanilla ice cream
1 pint strawberry ice cream
1 pint pistachio ice cream
1 cup heavy cream (whipped to stiff peaks)
1/2 cup candied cherries (chopped)
Ice cream mold or other mold dish

Put ice cream mold into the freezer. In a large bowl, beat vanilla ice cream until smooth, not melted. Spread vanilla ice cream into

chilled mold and freeze until firm. Next, beat strawberry ice cream until smooth, and spread over the vanilla. Again freeze until firm. Then beat pistachio ice cream until smooth, and spread over the strawberry. Freeze again. In a medium bowl, stir whipped cream and cherries together until well blended. Once mold is frozen well together, slice into wedges and serve with whipped cream mixture on the top. This dessert is a very patriotic one for Italians, in that the colors of the ice cream are the three colors of the flag of Italy.

The month of October, is recognized by the United States Federal Government as Italian Heritage Month. This is a time to recognize and celebrate the contributions of Italian Americans. One of the most recognized Italians during this month, would obviously be Christopher Columbus, who is recognized for being America's founding father.

Miscellaneous

The following recipes are those
that don't quite fit into a specific
category, but are foods and drink
commonly eaten and enjoyed by
Italians. Many of these recipes
can be enjoyed as snacks at
various times throughout the
day, or on special occasions

PIZZA PIENA

This is the popular "Ham Pie" or "Meat Pie" that most Italians serve around the Easter holiday. It is not usually part of the meal, but is served at breakfast or as a snack, or with an array of desserts. It is tradition for Italians to make this pie and bring some of it to any family members or friends they would visit over the holiday. So don't be surprised if you go to an Italian's home on Easter and find 5 versions of this delicious pie. This recipe makes 2 pies.

Crust:
5 cups flour
1 cup shortening
1 teaspoon baking powder
1 teaspoon salt
Water (as needed)
Filling: (the following meats should be cut from a deli in 1/4" slabs)
1 pound Proscuitto Ham
1 pound Dry Sausage
1/2 pound Salami
1/2 pound Ham
1 pound Ricotta cheese
1 pound Basket cheese
16 eggs
2 teaspoons pepper

PIZZA PIENA (con't)

Crust: In a large bowl, mix all above ingredients, adding water until the dough is soft and pliable (not sticky). Knead dough well. Roll out onto a floured surface. Place dough crusts into deep dishes (about 8" in diameter and 3" high). Rolled out dough must cover bottom and sides of dish. Reserve some dough for the top two crusts.

Filling: Cut all meats and basket cheese into very small cubes. Place meat in a large mixing bowl. In a small bowl, beat eggs. Add eggs to meat mixture, then add Ricotta cheese and pepper. Stir until well blended. Pour meat mixtures into dishes. Cover each dish with top crust. Seal well and trim excess dough. Be sure to press down with fork around and prick top of crust with fork prongs to allow to breathe. Brush the top of the crusts with a slightly beaten egg. Bake at 450 degrees for half an hour, then turn

to 400 degrees for a half hour more. Allow to cool, and serve warm, not hot.

If someone you know is having a housewarming party and either they or yourself are of Italian heritage, a 'traditional Italian housewarming gift' would be a perfect choice of something to bring. This gift consists of a basket of bread, wine and salt, with each having a symbolic meaning. The bread is so the homeowner may never go hungry, the wine so they may never go thirsty and the salt is to mend all wounds. This thoughtful gift would sure be the talk of the party.

DANDELION WINE

1 quart Dandelion blossoms
3 pounds sugar
2 oranges; sliced, not peeled
1 lemon; sliced, not peeled
1/2 package cake yeast
1 gallon water

Take Dandelions, break off stems and wash blossoms thoroughly.
Place in a large bowl. In a large saucepan, boil 1 gallon water.
Pour water over blossoms, and let stand for at least 2 hours. Strain
through cheese cloth back into the pan. Add sugar and return liquid
to a boil. Boil uncovered 4 minutes. Let stand until lukewarm. Add
the cake yeast, oranges and lemon, mix well. Let stand for 24
hours. Strain again through cheesecloth and bottle. At least 6
weeks aging is necessary. The longer it stands the better it is. Be
sure to store in a cool, dark place.

*Every year, my great grandmother Marguerite would be in
charge of making the dandelion wine, and from stories I've
heard, she would many times make so many bottles, they
would need to be stored in 'the boiler room' (where the
furnace was). And during the aging process of the wine, my
mother could recall many times hearing loud pops and finding
the bottles of wine that had exploded during the
fermentation... so the moral of the story... be sure to store the
wine in a cool, dark place.*

PIZZA DOUGH

Pizza means "pie" in Italian. This is a circular fresh bread dough, that can be served with a variety of toppings from vegetables to meat to even some types of fish.

1 package dried yeast (1/4 ounce)
1 1/3 cup lukewarm water
2 tablespoons olive oil
1 teaspoon salt
4 cups sifted flour

In a large bowl, dissolve yeast with lukewarm water. Add oil, then flour and salt to mixture. Knead until smooth (about 10 minutes). Cover bowl with cloth or wax paper and put in a warm place until double in bulk (about 2 hours). Place dough on 2 greased round pizza pans(12"), pizza stones or on a greased cookie sheet. Flatten and stretch dough with oiled fingers. Cover with your favorite toppings (always use sauce first, then Mozzarella cheese, then you may add sausage, mushrooms, anchovies, broccoli, etc...). Bake at 425 degrees for 20 minutes until crispy. The dough should be golden brown and hardened underneath.

The famous Italian delicacy, the pizza, originated in Naples, and is now popular all over the world. It was created for a visit from the Queen of Italy, Margherita, in 1889, and consisted of dough topped with the colors of Italy's flag. Tomatoes for red, Basil for green and Mozzarella for white.

INDIVIDUAL CALZONES

1 batch of Pizza dough
1/2 pound Ricotta cheese
8 ounce package Mozzarella cheese
1/4 cup grated Parmesan cheese
4 tablespoons oregano
2 tomatoes (diced)
Salt & Pepper (season to taste)
Marinara sauce (if desired)

Prepare pizza dough according to directions on page 120. Once dough has risen, place on a floured surface and knead for about 3 minutes. Divide dough into 4 pieces and roll out each into 1/4" thick round pieces. Place each piece of dough on a greased cookie sheet. In a large bowl, mix all above ingredients except Marinara sauce until well blended. Place about 1/4 cup of mixture onto center of dough. Brush some water on the edges of dough to aid in the sticking, then fold the dough over to form a turnover shape. Pinch edges, so none of the filling can leak out. Bake at 400

degrees for 15 minutes or until golden brown on both sides. Serve with Marinara sauce for dunking. Garnish with Parmesan cheese. *You can also add a variety of fresh vegetables (such as zucchini,broccoli,squash, etc...) or meats (ground beef, sausage) if you desire. However, before adding the vegetable to the cheese mixture, you must saute vegetable in olive oil until soft, since baking time is not ample enough to cook vegetables through.

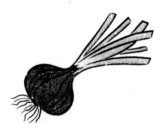

SWEET PEPPER AND ONION SANDWICHES

2 red peppers (sliced longways)
1 yellow pepper (sliced longways)
1 medium onion (sliced in strips)
1/4 cup olive oil
4 ounces shredded Mozzarella cheese
1 teaspoon oregano
Salt & Pepper to taste
1 loaf Italian bread

In a large skillet, warm olive oil over medium heat. Add peppers and saute for 10 minutes. Add onion, oregano, and salt and pepper,

and cook for an additional 10 minutes. Once vegetables are softened, place on loaf of Italian bread. Sprinkle Mozzarella cheese over the peppers, and place Italian bread under the broiler until cheese melts and is a golden brown. Serve hot.

In Italy during the Christmas season, Nativity scenes are on display every where. The manger scene originated in Italy and was first made by Saint Francis of Assisi. This scene consists usually of a stable with statues of Mary, Joseph, Jesus Christ, the Three Wise Men and various farm animals. Each town usually has one in their center, while individual townspeople erect them on their front lawns. So don't be surprised if you enter an Italian American's home and see a Nativity scene set up

TOMATO AND CHEESE HERBED CROSTINI

1 loaf Italian bread (cut into 1/2" slices)
1/4 cup olive oil
2 cloves garlic (minced)
2 teaspoons oregano
2 plum tomatoes (diced)
1 cup shredded Mozzarella cheese

Preheat oven to 400 degrees. Arrange bread slices on a baking sheet. Brush with oil and bake until lightly toasted, about 5 minutes. Meanwhile, in a small bowl, mix tomatoes, oregano and garlic. Place about 1 tablespoon of this mixture on each piece of bread. Top with shredded Mozzarella cheese. Return to oven, and bake for 7 minutes or until cheese is melted and bubbly. Serve warm.

Quotes by Famous Italians

"I'm gonna make him an offer he can't refuse".... *Marlon Brando* (as Don Vito Corleone in 'The Godfather')

"It's like deja vu all over again"

"It ain't over til it's over"

"Baseball is 90% mental and the other half is physical"

"Slump? I ain't in no slump I just ain't hitting"..... infamous 'Yogiisms' by baseball great *Yogi Berra*

"Do every act as if it were your last"....*Marcus Aurelius*

"I came I saw I conquered"....*Julius Caesar*

"You cannot teach a man anything; you can only help him find it within himself"....*Galileo Galilei*

ITALIAN COMBO SANDWICH

1/4 pound salami
1/4 pound ham
1/4 pound Italian roast beef
1/4 pound Provolone cheese
1 12 ounce loaf Focaccia bread
1/4 cup of Italian salad dressing
Romaine lettuce

Cut Focaccia bread crosswise in half. Brush both sides generously with salad dressing. Layer meats and cheese on bread and top with some Romaine lettuce. Some roasted peppers are also a delicious addition to this sandwich. Return top half of bread to sandwich and cut into 4 wedges. If you are unable to find Focaccia bread, regular Italian bread is a tasty substitution.

> One of the most famous structures in all of Italy, is 'The Leaning Tower of Pisa'. This spectacular sight was first started in 1173 by architect Bonanno Pisano, and was completed some 150 years later in 1350 by Giovanni di Simone. The softness of the soil on this site, and partial sinking of the foundation is what created this beautiful mistake of a masterpiece.

TUNA STUFFED PLUM TOMATOES

2 6 ounce cans white albacore tuna fish
6 large plum tomatoes
1/4 cup mayonnaise
4 basil leaves (minced)
1 stalk celery (diced)
1/2 cup Mozzarella cheese
1/4 cup Italian seasoned bread crumbs
1/4 cup olive oil

TUNA STUFFED PLUM TOMATOES (con't)

Clean tomatoes well. Cut 1/4" off the top of tomatoes and clean out seeds and majority of pulp, so shell of the tomato is remaining. In a small bowl, mix mayonnaise, tuna, celery, 1/4 cup of Mozzarella cheese and seasonings. Mix well. Stuff each of the tomatoes with tuna mixture. Sprinkle remainder of Mozzarella cheese over the tuna. Then sprinkle a little bread crumbs over cheese. Drizzle olive oil over each tomato. Bake at 400 degrees for 15 minutes. Serve warm or hot.

Now That's Italian!

Italy can take credit for creating some of the many popular and talented individuals of the 20th century. Whether born in America from immigrant parents, or in Italy, the following individuals are not known for their accomplishments alone, but for their Italian heritage as well

Madonna: singer and actress who became popular in the 1980's

Sophia Loren: the beautiful Italian born actress

Frank Sinatra: 'Old Blue Eyes'; one of the most revered singers of all time

Joe DiMaggio: 'The Yankee Clipper'; popular baseball player

Rocky Marciano: 'The Brockton Blockbuster'; famous boxer

Luciano Pavorotti: one of the greatest tenors of all time

Martin Scorsese: one of the most respected filmmakers

Rudy Guiliani: the beloved former mayor of New York City

James Gandolfini: the popular mob boss Tony Soprano on 'The Soprano's'

and finally...**Immaculata DelPreto Simeone**...my grandmother; the heart and soul of our family, who inspired many of the recipes in this book

---

ITALIAN QUICHE

1 cup Swiss cheese
4 eggs
1 can artichoke hearts (drained & diced)
1 cup heavy cream
1 12 ounce bag spinach (cooked, drained & chopped)
1/4 teaspoon salt
1 tablespoon butter
1 clove garlic (minced)

Preheat oven to 400 degrees. In a small skillet, warm butter and saute garlic on low heat until softened. In a medium bowl, toss garlic, artichokes, spinach and cheese. Mix well. Spread mixture into a greased casserole dish. In a small bowl, wisk eggs, cream and salt. Pour over mixture. Bake uncovered for 35 minutes.

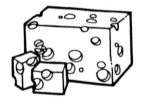

PEPPER, POTATO AND EGG SUBS

According to my grandmother, this was a popular dish for Italian American immigrants during the depression. These foods were relatively easy to get and an inexpensive dish to make.

3 large green peppers (sliced longways)
4 large potatoes (peeled & diced)
8 eggs
1/2 cup olive oil
2 teaspoons oregano
1 1/2 teaspoons salt
1 teaspoon pepper

In a medium pan, bring 5 cups water and potatoes to a boil. Reduce heat and allow to boil lightly for about 10 minutes, until just soft. Drain, pat dry and set aside. In a large skillet, warm olive oil on medium heat. Add green peppers and saute about 12 minutes. Add potatoes and cook for another 10 minutes or until both peppers and potatoes are soft. In a small bowl, wisk eggs, oregano, salt and pepper. Add mixture to skillet. Cook for about 5 more minutes, or until eggs are well cooked and starting to brown. Slice Italian bread longways, and add mixture. Serve hot.

In Italy, every village and town has a 'piazza'. This location is similar to a town green in America, however, this central meeting place is used on a daily basis by Italians as a place to mingle and socialize with friends and relatives.

PORTABELLO MUSHROOM SANDWICHES

4 portabello mushroom caps (sliced)
1 large red onion (cut in rounds)
1/4 cup marsala wine
3 tablespoons olive oil
1/4 cup mayonnaise
3 basil leaves (chopped)
4 slices Provolone cheese
4 Italian hard rolls

In a medium skillet, warm olive oil over medium heat. Saute onion for about 7 minutes or until tender. Remove onions and set aside. Add portabello mushrooms and marsala wine and saute for about 10 minutes. Remove from pan and set aside. In a small bowl, mix mayonnaise and basil. On each roll, layer mushroom, onion and piece of Provolone cheese. Place under broiler to just melt cheese. Once cheese is melted, spread some of the mayonnaise mixture on each roll and serve.

Growing up, most Italians are taught that when they are invited into someone's home for a meal, they must bring a gift for the host or hostess. This gift is usually a bottle of wine, a loaf of Italian bread to serve with dinner, or a dessert to be eaten after the meal.

HAM AND CHEESE LOAF

6 slices bacon (diced)
6 eggs
3/4 cup milk
1 1/2 cup flour
2 1/2 teaspoons baking powder
1 cup Monterey Jack cheese (shredded)
1 cup Cheddar cheese (shredded)
1 cup ham or proscuitto (cubed)

In a small skillet, brown bacon until light and golden over medium heat. Drain on towel paper. In a large bowl, beat eggs until light and foamy. Add milk until smooth, then stir in remaining ingredients and blend well. Pour mixture into a greased and floured 9x5 loaf pan. Bake in a preheated oven at 350 degrees for 50-60 minutes until golden brown.

One of the most aggravating things for myself, my sisters and my cousins while growing up, was when our grandparents would suddenly begin talking Italian so we would not understand what they were saying. It was during those heated discussions that the language would change, the voices would become louder and the hands would begin to move rapidly that we would listen intently to get any sense of what was being said....always to no avail....

FRESELLA

3 1/2 cups flour
1 1/2 teaspoons salt
1 teaspoon pepper
3/4 cup vegetable oil
1 cup cold water

In a large bowl, mix all above ingredients together well. Take about a fistful of dough at a time and roll out onto a floured surface to the shape of a rope. You will then cut this into 1" bite size pieces. Place on an ungreased cookie sheet and bake for 30 minutes on 350 degrees. This will make about 100 - 125. These pepper biscuits are used many times as a topping in soup, as a little snack or with a side of coffee.

Before things were considered 'politically incorrect', in many Italian households, the liquor Brandy seemed to be a "cure-all" for a variety of 'ailments'. The baby's teething....give her a little Brandy, the kid won't go to sleep.... give him a little Brandy, the children have a bad cold....give them a little Brandy. I don't hear too much of this anymore, but there was definitely a time when Italians used their Brandy as a home remedy.

HERBED GARLIC BREAD

1/2 cup parsley
1 teaspoon thyme
2 cloves garlic (minced)
1/2 teaspoon salt
1/4 teaspoon pepper
2 tablespoons olive oil
2 tablespoons butter (melted)
1 12 ounce package shredded Mozzarella cheese
1 loaf Italian bread

Preheat oven to broil. In a small bowl, wisk together all above ingredients. Cut bread longways 3/4 of the way through. Brush herb mixture liberally on each side, then top with Mozzarella cheese. Broil bread until cheese is melted, stringy and golden brown, watching closely, as not to burn. Cut into slices 3/4 way through, so the bread is still intact. Place in a bread basket and serve warm.

> In Italy, the main meal is served at mid-day. At this time of day, virtually everything closes down, (except of course restaurants) and remain closed for about 3 hours so Italians can enjoy their favorite past time.....enjoying food and sharing it with family and friends. Obviously, food is an important part of the Italian culture and lifestyle and is used as a tool to unite and bring individuals together for a common purpose; to 'break bread', as they say, with those we cherish most in our lives

Acknowledgements

Camaraderie, fellowship and pride are just a few of the words used to describe the way Italians feel about their culture. Being raised in a community where Italians held their heritage like a badge of honor, the traditions and signatures of the Italian lifestyle became ingrained early on. The town of East Haven, Connecticut where I grew up was reported in the year 2002 to have the second largest population of Italians per capita in the country. So inevitably, in this atmosphere made up predominately of individuals with Italian roots, things such as family, friends and of course cooking were deemed extremely important.

The inspiration for this cookbook came from the countless family members and friends whose love for cooking, and pride in Italian heritage and traditions made me want to share these wonderful recipes while also giving a little insight into the Italian lifestyle. The majority of the recipes in this cookbook originated from the Campagnia region in Southern Italy, which to many would be considered the 'Neapolitan' way of cooking.

Special thanks to the late Immaculata DelPreto Simeone, Teresa Falcigno and Carmel Masotta, Patricia Gagne and Donna Miconi who shared some of their famous recipes to be included in this book. Many of these recipes have been shared for generations and hopefully will be carried on for years to come.

Index of Recipes

Italian Culture Index

Growing Up Italian

The memories of ones childhood definitely last a lifetime. My memories are full of friends, family, food, tradition and the neighborhood. In our neighborhood, virtually everyone was Italian...or at least wanted to be. I lived on a little street in East Haven, CT, right by the shore. My grandmother and grandfather lived right across the street and my aunt, uncle and cousins around the corner. We were surrounded by the Zito's, Limoncelli's, Esposito's, Musco's & Gaetano's; just to name a few. Everyone knew everyone, and we were all connected with the bond of our heritage. The commonality of Italian traits was also apparent there on Philip Street. Neighbors were loud (you could hear many a marital tiff), kids could be 'fresh', and there were those who were

real 'cafones'. But all in all, we had pride in who we were and our deep roots, and respected each other.

On our street, there were kids, kids everywhere. We would play, and our parents would watch and gossip about whoever wasn't there. Everyone had a vegetable garden, and they would share their fresh summer bounty with each other. There were even some chickens and goats hidden in some yards. We would see gramma and grandpa everyday, and all day long in the summer and on weekends. In the summer we would go to mass each morning, we would then come home, pick something from the garden and cook. My grandmother was a great cook, and no one could wait until Sunday afternoon. Sunday was always family day, and all aunts, uncles and cousins would jam pack into their small, humble home, but no one seemed to mind, as long as we were all together.

Eventually, as our immediate family got larger, it was time to move about 1/4 of a mile away to our new larger home. Trust me,

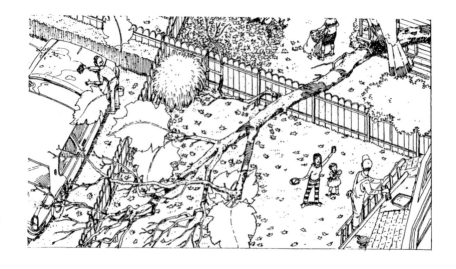

it was very traumatic for us all. We were now surrounded by the Mascola's, Russo's, Lucatino's & Alberino's. At that time, half of them could not speak a word of English and to this day, still can't. On our first day in our new home, in true Italian style 'Cookie' Alberino, our new next door neighbor had us over for dinner. I remember looking around her beautiful home in awe; she had big hair, long painted nails and she even had an aquarium in the wall...not to mention she was a great cook.

In school, it was pretty much the same. I had 12 years of Catholic education (so did my cousins and 2 of them graduated from high school, and entered the convent...they virtually opened the gates of Heaven for the whole family, and of course my grandmother couldn't be happier). All of my friends were Italian, but then again there wasn't really much choice since that's all there was. My best friend was Maria Acampora; she was great. Her family was Maria her mom, dad John and brother John. Every Sunday her parents would have front row seats at church, they worked the festival at the church in the summer, and were just a true family. And Maria was just a true friend. They all always insisted that her grandmother haunted their house, and obviously in some way kept them all together.

Aside from school and the neighborhood though, it was like a rite of passage for all Italian girls to take dance at some point in their life. This is where you can witness the relationships between Italian women first hand. My sisters and I went to "Steppin' Out" dancing studio, run by Donna Lombardi, an ex-Rockette. Donna was the classic Italian woman...loud, funny, blunt, she loved being in the mix of it all and loved to gossip. I can remember the laughs we had, many times at the expense of others, but always in good fun. It was pretty much just an extension of our actual families, we all treated each other like family. We traveled together like family, to the Poconos, New Jersey, Tap O Mania in New York and our claim to fame; we danced on "The Costa Riviera" Italian cruise

line. The relationships among Italian women run deep. Even if you may not see each other in forever, when you're reunited it's as if you never left each other's sides. But these relationships can go two ways....when you're a friend, you're a friend for life...but if you damage that relationship, you could be written off for life. Italian women are very passionate about their beliefs, their family and friends; we may be stubborn at times, but we live our lives as straight shooters with conviction.

It was not until I moved away to college that I suddenly felt out of my element. There, my Boston-born Irish friends would harass me about my grammar and inability to talk quietly, among other things. I thought everyone said things such as "What are you's doing?". I guess not, but it was eye-opening to see others who felt just as passionate about their heritage and customs....I must say there is no better place to be than in the heart of Boston (with the Lucy family) on St. Patrick's Day. Erin Go Braugh!

Now as an adult it's still the same...I have a friend at work who's also Italian and we were hysterical when we had identical stories of teachers in grade school telling our parents to please have our hearing checked because we were so loud. It's a cultural thing...don't they know? But now the difference is I have children that I want to cherish their Italian heritage. I make sauce most Sundays, and my son rolls the little meatballs for him and his sister. We plant a huge garden in the summer, and we sing songs in Italian that were sang to me as a child, and are now some of my children's favorites.

As I look back now, being Italian in not just a culture, but a way of life. And it is that life that I love to look back on and recall... Gino's Apizza, The Avest on Wooster Street, eating platters of antipasto, the Calabro cheese factory down the street, Gramma's garden, friends from Steppin' Out, dancing at St. Anthony's annual feast, Sunday dinners of macaronni and meatballs, our fish feast on

Christmas Eve, our Friday night pasta e fagioli dinners, sitting under the dining room table while gramma and grandpa played cards with their 'comares' and pretty much everything about the old neighborhood.

When my great grandparents were carried over the Atlantic 'on the boat', from their little Southern Italian towns, they not only

brought with them their traditions and heritage, they brought a tremendous amount of passion, great aspirations for their families and most of all pride. These Italians wanted to be Americans, but still wanted to hold onto who they were culturally. They wanted their children to have the American dream, but to never lose sight of where they came from. Fortunately, for my children, they have my mother who is a second generation Italian and my father in-law who is a first generation Italian, to get the true sense of how it was to grow up Italian.

It was shortly after I returned home from college, that my grandparents passed away. It was at this time that things slowly began to change; the glue that held our family together suddenly became unstuck. Those Sunday dinners and Christmas Eve feasts were now celebrated among immediate family members. Nowadays, we see the extended family of aunts, uncles and countless cousins on "occasions" and not just for the hell of it. But then again, we all have families of our own now, the next generation of memory makers. And I am sure that for all of us, we will pass on those childhood memories and traditions, and how it really was growing up Italian in the hopes that our own children will cherish the same.

An Italian Christmas &
The Tale of the Fishes

The Christmas season is a wonderful mixture of fabulous sights, breathtaking smells and harmonious sounds. Whether it be the ground blanketed with snow, the intoxicating aromas of tomato sauce simmering on the stove, or the glorious sounds of Frank Sinatra singing a Christmas hymn, all of these things evoke memories of Christmas past and allows us to yearn for the many traditions and customs that we come to associate with this festive holiday.

Since Christmas is said to have originated in Italy in 274 A.D., it is obviously a very important holiday for many Italians. The popular colors of Christmas (red & green) came from the colors of the flag, and it was the Franciscan friar St Francis of Assisi who introduced the Christmas carol, as well as the nativity (creche) scene. For Christian Italians, the weeks leading up to Christmas are filled with preparation and anticipation. This is the time that Italians get ready for the 2 day feast on Christmas Eve and Christmas Day; making cookies, pies & breads in advance, checking so that all ingredients are on hand for their traditional menu, and making sure the comforts of home will be felt by all who enter. Italian family life in general usually revolves around faith, family, friends and food, so for an Italian, when the Christmas season is in full swing these important aspects of life are multiplied.

Although both Christmas Eve and Christmas Day are important holidays for Italians, Christmas Eve is definately the more celebrated of the two. For my family, on this evening we indulge in our fish feast. "La Viglia Napoletana" is a Southern Italian tradition in which individuals eat only fish on Christmas Eve. This tradition is not observed by all Italians, but is generally celebrated from Rome to the South. The tradition of eating fish on Christmas Eve generally came from it being a day of abstinence where the early Catholic church prohibited the eating meat on this day.

Many families have different traditions on the set number of fish dishes they serve on this festive holiday, and that number usually has some religious significance. The number of dishes run anywhere from 3-12, with the number representing the following: The number 3 signifies the trinity, having 4 fish dishes represents the 4 gospels, 5 signifies the number of wounds Christ suffered on the cross. The number 7 can signify both the 7 sacraments or the 7 utterances Jesus Christ made from the cross. 9 represents the 9 months of Mary's pregnancy, and 12 refers to the number of Christ's apostles. There are still countless other reasons for the number of fish individuals serve on this festive holiday.

However, we must remember, Italian appetites cannot survive on fish alone, so in addition to all the fish, there are countless side dishes to accompany the meal. From antipasto, to the lasagna, to the countless platters of marinated vegetables and cheeses, food is usually the core of the holiday gathering, used to unite families. This traditional holiday means so much to so many, but aside from the many aromas and tastes to be had, the part of this feast that is so meaningful, is the true togetherness it brings among families. And as we exchange gifts with loved ones, we must remember that the best present we can give our families is our treasured customs and traditions.

So, when the hustle and bustle of the holiday season is finally over, a sense of both relief and sadness emerge. As the tiny icicles hanging on the eaves glisten outside, the aromas from the Christmas feast still linger in the air, and we look at the dimly lit manger, one cannot help but yearn for that feeling that Christmas brings to all families.

Please Pass the Vino

As many well know, Italians love their wine. They love to smell it, they love to make it, they love to savor it, and most of all they love to drink it. You can say, Italians just have a love affair with wine. There are many Italian Americans that can recall the distinct taste of their Poppy's homemade wine. Italians take great pride in creating their own home made wine and cannot wait until fall comes, the end of harvest season, to begin the tedious ritual of wine creation. I have heard countless stories of how my husband's grandfather, in particular, used his wine as many a resource.... So, with this beverage being such a large part of Italian culture, there are surely some traditions and stories that go along with it.

Traditionally, wine is served with most evening meals in an Italian household. It was always an exciting time for the older Italian males to be the first to give a sip of 'vino' to their grandson's

even at a very young age....almost as a rite of passage. My husband can recall this, and how delicious his grandfather's wine was, especially when mixed with orange soda.

Wine is also used as a tool to celebrate and reunite. When my Uncle Joe was 17 years old in 1943, he joined the Marine Corps to serve his country. Upon his return, in true Italian style, his father took him to the basement, which had a dirt floor instead of cement. He knew right where to dig to find a bottle of homemade wine of a special vintage to toast his homecoming.

For others, wine is just a part of their daily life. For my great-grandfather Frank Simeone, his wine *was* his life. Every October, like clockwork, he would be busy in his cellar, mashing his grapes for his yearly supply of homemade wine. He enjoyed, from what I hear, 3 glasses of wine an evening with dinner. Well, as he got older, there became times when he wasn't

feeling so great. So finally, his wife Marguerite convinced him to go see the doctor. The doctor inquired about his diet and such. Grandpa Frank easily told him about his love of wine and the 3 glasses he consumed each evening. The doctor then made a recommendation to him to cut back on his wine to maybe only one glass per evening. He reluctantly agreed, and decided from then on out to have only one glass per evening. So, as the family sat down to dinner that very evening, something at the table appeared a little different...Grandpa certainly took the advice of the doctor to only drink one glass of wine; but of course his typical wine glass disappeared and what showed up in its place was a 32 ounce mug to hold his prized, delicious vino.

And finally, there are those who take great pride in sharing their yearly creation with everyone around them. My father-in-law tells stories of how his father 'christened' his friends when they would come to their home. If Grandpa Miconi liked you, you would be brought down to the cellar to try some of his wine. And not a just a sip or two, but usually a few glasses. And if you have ever tried homemade wine, you're well aware of the quickly numbing effects it can have on any individual. If you were able to stay and drink the wine, you passed the first part of the test, and if you were able to make it back up the stairs on your own accord, you passed the second part of the test and you were 'in'; however, if you required some assistance getting out of the cellar, let's just say, that would be the last time you were invited downstairs.

You know you're Italian when.....

⁺Your grandparents pronounce Italy: It lee and bottle: bot el

*You have at least one relative that has entered the convent or monastery

*You have male cousins named Anthony, Louie, Mario or Dominic and female
cousins named Mary, Marie, Carmel or Louisa

*By age 5 you knew you could not eat until Poppy was sitting down at the
dinner table

*Your grandfather makes his own wine

*He then takes you by the age of 7 to hide under the grapevines in the back yard
to try a sip...or maybe two

*You thought everyone talked loud and at the same time

*You have been threatened with a wooden spoon

*You are told to preserve your old nylons to tie up tomato plants in the summer
or to strain paint through

*The men in your family get together to play cards in the garage

*Your grandmother has tried to carry over the tradition of eating fish on Fridays
during Lent to every Friday during the year

*You have statues of Mary and Jesus, and rosaries throughout your home

*You grow all your own vegetables in the summer especially tomatoes
and zucchini, and always bring the extras to family and friends

*All year long, you wait for those summer time squash flower patties

*You have just fried meatballs for breakfast on Sundays

*Your favorite movies include The Godfather, Goodfellas and A Bronx Tale

*Your grandmother washes out plastic bags and re-uses them

*You are related to at least one electrician, mechanic, plumber and painter

*You live within an 1/8 mile radius of much of your family - with at least 3
relatives living on your street

*Your best friends growing up were your cousins, and even now

*You had about 20 people in your wedding party

*You know all the words to "That's Amore" and "Volare"

*Your grandmother refuses to take the plastic off the furniture in the parlor

*You would never order a sauce dish at a restaurant

*Your really big family gatherings were in the garage

*You have been hit by a nun at least once

*Your grandmother was named after a holy day or a Saint

*You can not talk without moving your hands

*Your aunts have nicknames like Cookie, Honey and Candy

*You or one of your male relatives have owned or wanted to own a Camero

*Your father may have $100,000 in the bank, but still duct tapes his slippers

*You can recite lines ver batem from The Soprano's and The Godfather

*You have said "I'll make him an offer he can't refuse" at least once in your life

*Christmas Eve is by far the social event of the year

*When company comes over there is always an antipasto on the table

*You aunt makes the sign of the cross and says 'Jesus, Mary & Joseph' when
  upset

*You have to have Anisette or Sambuca with your espresso

*You eat dinner at 2:00 on Sundays

*Your grandfather grows fig trees

*You've called someone a "mamaluke", a "puttana" or a "stunod"

*You own a gold chain with a cross, a horn...and maybe even a pinky ring

*You can pronounce ricotta, manicotti and mozzarella the right way

*All of your friends last names end in a vowel

*You have a least one relative who had to "go away for a little while", and your
  grandmother can't understand why everyone is always picking on him

*You grandparents save everything to use more than once, and duct tape is
  considered one of the greatest inventions of the 20th century

*Your neighbor has a white Christmas tree with pink lights

*Frank Sinatra, Dean Martin, Tony Bennett and Louis Prima are loved and
  played daily

*Your theme song is "My Way"

*You have a list of numbers you can call to bet the horses

*Your mother acts like it's the end of the world then lays on a guilt trip if you
  miss a family dinner

*Your grandmother either doesn't have her license or got it when she turned 50

*The males in your family belong to an Italian social club

*When you're 30, your friends will still be those you had from your
  neighborhood when you were 10

*You've had at least one person fall into your tomato garden drunk snapping all
  your plants

Need A Gift?

For

- Shower • Birthday • Mother's Day
  - Anniversary • Christmas

Turn Page for Order Form
(Order Now While Supply Lasts!)

TO ORDER COPIES OF:
Le Ricette di un Villaggio Italiano
Please send me _____ copies at $11.95
each plus $2.25 S/H each. (Make checks
payable to **HEARTS N TUMMIES**.)

Name _____

Street _____

City _____ State _____ Zip _____

SEND ORDERS TO:
HEARTS N TUMMIES
3544 Blakslee St.
Wever IA   52658
800-571-2665

TO ORDER COPIES OF:
Le Ricette di un Villaggio Italiano
Please send me _____ copies at $11.95
each plus $2.25 S/H each. (Make checks
payable to **HEARTS N TUMMIES**.)

Name _____

Street _____

City _____ State _____ Zip _____

SEND ORDERS TO:
HEARTS N TUMMIES
3544 Blakslee St.
Wever IA   52658
800-571-2665